Confronting the Threat

A Guide to Reducing Domestic and Gun Violence

Aubin M Jack Sr.

Dedication

Dedicated to the United States of America. May we all live together in harmony.

Preface

"In America's gun violence 'epidemic', Oxford High in Michigan is the **28th school shooting of 2021**"

"Tourist shot dead protecting his baby from attack by gunman 'on mushrooms' in Florida"

"Female high school wrestling star shot dead in Chicago after Halloween shopping trip"

Every day, 106 Americans are killed and over 200 are injured by firearms. Americans should be outraged because this type of horror should never be acceptable in a civilized society. It's time that "We the People of the United States" stand together to confront the daily threats of gun violence before it becomes an uncontrollable epidemic.

Unfortunately, the facts show that we need to act soon.

"The Small Arms Survey stated that U.S. civilians alone account for 393 million (about 46 percent) of the worldwide total of civilian-held firearms. This amounts to **120.5 firearms for every 100 residents**."

If that's not alarming, how about these facts:

"An abuser's access to a firearm increases the risk of femicide by at least 400%."

"Women in the U.S. are 11 times more likely to be murdered with a gun than in other high-income nations."[1]

---

[1] Anon. n.d. "NCADV | National Coalition Against Domestic Violence." Retrieved January 18, 2022 (https://ncadv.org/STATISTICS).

It's clear that we are experiencing a record level of gun and domestic violence in America. However, the violence and deaths in our streets, neighborhoods, and homes will increase exponentially if we continue to legislate with "Band-Aid solutions". We must act now and pass common-sense gun laws, like the ones addressed by the Violence Project, to protect our people from the unimaginable carnage that's quickly approaching. Did you know that researchers from this project concluded last February that 146 out of 167 mass shootings since 1996 could have been avoided? "This includes all but one mass shootings in the last five years."[2]

Here are the five common-sense gun laws advocated by this group that can save the lives of law enforcement and Americans right now. It will make all of us safer and more accountable.

- Establish mandatory universal background checks

- Keep firearms away from violent and suicidal people

- Need safe storage of firearms and ammo

- Ban assault weapons

- Prohibit buying a gun for another person

---

[2] Mukherjee, Rahul. 2020. "How Many Mass Shootings Might Have Been Prevented by Stronger Gun Laws?" *Los Angeles Times.* Retrieved January 18, 2022 (https://www.latimes.com/projects/if-gun-laws-were-enacted/).

Contents

Chapter 1: Introduction

Close your eyes and consider yourself transported back to the crime-ridden streets of New York in the late 1980s. Violent crime was a public health emergency. The first and most obvious consequence was the toll it took on individuals and communities – the lost lives of the bereaved families, the traumatized children, the fleeing families, and shuttered businesses, leaving inequality and joblessness for those who were left behind.

Crime Statistics in the U.S.

The United States is experiencing its most violent period in the twenty-first century. Americans are witnessing an unprecedented crime wave. After decades of decline, shootings have increased in recent years. In the middle of a pandemic, gun deaths in the United States hit an all-time high in 2020.

Despite the fact that experts cannot declare anything certain about total crime in 2021, shooting occurrences look to be on the rise in several regions. We've also seen a number of mass shootings, including the murder of spa and massage employees in the Atlanta area and a grocery store massacre in Boulder, Colorado.

As we did ten years ago, Americans can no longer claim that we are living in the safest period in our country's history. Why crime rises and diminishes is a perplexing topic. Few individuals have given it as much attention as Patrick Sharkey, a sociologist at Princeton University. While others seek simple solutions and catchy slogans, Sharkey embraces complexity and unpredictability. In his 2018 book, *Uneasy Peace*, Sharkey argues that intense and harsh policing and jail practices likely helped cut crime in recent decades to the great benefit of low-income neighborhoods. However, rather than glorifying these measures, they required ruthless policing techniques that could spark a societal backlash — hence the "uneasy" aspect of the peace.

Last year, the United States had its highest spike in murder rates in decades. Even while the general crime rate fell, the expected total number of killings increased to levels not seen since the late 1990s. So far, the increase has persisted through 2021. According to data from U.S. cities, homicides are up about 15% this year compared to the same period last year.[3]

The surge in killings and shootings is reflected not only in statistics but also in actual incidents. During the month of July 2021, the sound of gunfire frightened baseball players and fans at Washington, DC's Nationals stadium. The mayor of Washington, DC, had denounced a drive-by shooting that killed a six-year-old the night before. Meanwhile, 11 people were killed, and 49 were injured in a total of 12 mass shootings from coast to coast.

Year-to-year changes in crime and violence are possible and do happen. However, the magnitude of the increase in murders has drawn larger public attention. The rise in homicides appears

---

[3] Lopez, German. 2021. "Murders Are up. Crime Is Not. What's Going on?" *Vox.* Retrieved January 18, 2022 (https://www.vox.com/22578430/murder-crime-2020-2021-covid-19-pandemic).

to be a distinctly American phenomenon. While murder rates grew in some wealthy countries last year, such as Canada and Germany, the increases were significantly lower than the double-digit rises seen in the United States. This is especially noteworthy, given that, after correcting for population, the United States already had a higher baseline of murders.

The stakes are really high. According to preliminary estimates, about 21,000 individuals were murdered in the United States in 2020. Another 10% increase or more could result in thousands of more deaths by 2021.

From the 1970s to the 1990s, the United States experienced a significant increase in murders and other crimes. However, the country entered a period of peace beginning in the mid-1990s, with rates of murder, violence, and other types of crimes dropping by more than half by 2014. In 2015 and 2016, the murder rate climbed briefly before leveling out and dropping again.

According to Sharkey, the year 2020 was undoubtedly the most violent of the [21st] century, with homicides increasing by an estimated 25%. Multiple sources, including the FBI, Asher, other reports from the Council on Criminal Justice, and the University of Pennsylvania—run website City Crime Stats, also backed up these conclusions.

On the other hand, different types of crimes, such as shootings, aggravated assaults, and car thefts, have also increased, according to preliminary data. Nonetheless, violent crime in general increased at a considerably lower rate, if at all, as compared to murders, and total crime decreased, owing in part to a decrease in the majority of property offenses. With businesses closed and people remaining at home, there were fewer opportunities to perpetrate property crimes last year. Car theft, the one sort of property crime that has increased, is frequently conducted as part of a bigger, more serious crime. It's what criminologists call a "keystone offense", such as stealing a car to use in a drive-by shooting so the offenders can't be identified easily.

The U.S. Public's Perception of Crime

Americans have a tendency to believe that crime is on the rise. In 20 of 24 Gallup polls done since 1993, at least 60% of U.S. adults stated there is more crime than the previous year, despite a typically downward trend in national violent and property crime statistics for the majority of that time.[4]

Perceptions of increased crime in the United States are at their highest level since 1993. However, the most recent data came at the close of an extraordinary year. Since March 2020, the coronavirus pandemic has kept many Americans at home longer than usual, perhaps lowering traffic and foreigners in their neighborhoods.

Meanwhile, this past summer's racial justice protests – many of which were peaceful, but some escalated into violence, looting, and arson – may have produced the perception of

---

[4] Gramlich, John. n.d. "What the Data Says (and Doesn't Say) about Crime in the United States." *Pew Research Center*. Retrieved January 18, 2022 (https://www.pewresearch.org/fact-tank/2020/11/20/facts-about-crime-in-the-u-s/).

increasing crime in the United States as a whole. Whatever the cause, the simple fact is that Americans are fearful. Three out of ten people are concerned about walking alone at night in their neighborhood. Gallup has been asking since 1965, "Is there any place near where you live – that is, within a mile – where you would be afraid to stroll alone at night?"

Currently, 29 percent of Americans say they would be terrified to walk alone at night in their neighborhood.[5]

The Most and Least Prevalent Types of Crime!

Property crime is far more widespread in the United States than violent crime. The FBI reported 2,109.9 property crimes per 100,000 people in 2019, compared to 379.4 violent crimes per 100,000 people.

Larceny/theft was the most common property crime in 2019, followed by burglary and motor vehicle theft. Aggravated assault was the most common violent crime, followed by robbery, rape, and murder/non-negligent manslaughter.

The FBI tracks a somewhat different collection of offenses than BJS, but it finds similar broad patterns, with theft being the most prevalent type of property crime in 2019 and assault being the most common type of violent crime.[6]

---

[5] Gramlich, John. n.d. "What the Data Says (and Doesn't Say) about Crime in the United States." *Pew Research Center*. Retrieved January 18, 2022 (https://www.pewresearch.org/fact-tank/2020/11/20/facts-about-crime-in-the-u-s/).

[6] Gramlich, John. n.d. "What the Data Says (and Doesn't Say) about Crime in the United States." *Pew Research Center*. Retrieved January 18, 2022 (https://www.pewresearch.org/fact-tank/2020/11/20/facts-about-crime-in-the-u-s/).

According to a Major Cities Chiefs Association survey, 63 of the 66 largest police jurisdictions saw rises in at least one category of violent crime in 2020, including homicide, rape, robbery, and aggravated assault.[7]

How Bad Is It?

So, in terms of actual crime, how bad is it in the United States?

It's tough to know for sure. The Federal Bureau of Investigation (FBI) and the Bureau of Justice Statistics (BJS), the two principal sources of government crime statistics, both offer an incomplete picture, while efforts to improve them are underway.

The FBI releases annual statistics on crimes that have been reported to the authorities but not on those that have not. The FBI focuses on a small number of specific violent and property offenses, but not on many other sorts of crime, such as drug trafficking.

While the FBI's data is based on information from thousands of federal, state, county, local, and other law enforcement agencies, not all of them participate every year. The FBI received data from almost eight out of ten agencies in 2019, the most recent full-year available.[8]

---

[7] CNN, Emma Tucker and Peter Nickeas. n.d. "The US Saw Significant Crime Rise across Major Cities in 2020. And It's Not Letting Up." *CNN*. Retrieved January 18, 2022 (https://www.cnn.com/2021/04/03/us/us-crime-rate-rise-2020/index.html).

[8] Gramlich, John. n.d. "What the Data Says (and Doesn't Say) about Crime in the United States." *Pew Research Center*. Retrieved January 18, 2022

BJS, for its part, keeps track of crime by conducting a big annual poll of Americans aged 12 and up, in which they are asked if they had been the victim of a crime in the previous six months. This method has the advantage of capturing both reported and unreported offenses. However, the BJS survey has its limitations. It, like the FBI, focuses primarily on a few violent and property crimes while omitting other types of crime. Because the BJS data is based on victim interviews conducted after the event, it is unable to give information on one particularly high-profile sort of crime: murder.

Putting such concerns aside, comparing FBI and BJS figures side by side gives investigators, academics, and journalists a good picture of violent and property crime rates in the United States, as well as how they've changed over time.

What's Causing It?

We still don't know what's causing it.

The closest thing to a consensus I've found in speaking with experts regarding the cause of the murder surge is: it's complicated.

It is rather difficult to attribute any year-to-year change in violent crime statistics to a single cause, and homicides and shootings are a highly local occurrence that can surge for a variety of reasons. However, the rise in homicide rates across the country is unprecedented and far-reaching, as were the

---

(https://www.pewresearch.org/fact-tank/2020/11/20/facts-about-crime-in-the-u-s/).

pandemic and social movements that impacted every aspect of society last year.

Experts believe that a variety of factors may have contributed to the increase in homicides. This includes:

- Economic collapse

- Social anxiety as a result of a pandemic

- De-policing in major cities following protests calling for the abolition of police departments

- Shift in police resources from neighborhoods as a result of those protests

- The release of criminal defendants pre-trial to reduce the risk of COVID-19 spread in jails

Thus, probable explanations have come up repeatedly.

1) COVID-19: The coronavirus was a powerful factor in 2020 and may have influenced homicide rates. The pandemic halted measures that are likely to protect Americans against violence, including police, social services, and community-led activities. As companies and schools closed, certain people, particularly teen boys and young men, had more leisure time to stew over interpersonal strife.

However, much of the world, from Mexico to Canada to much of Europe, struggled with COVID-19 and did not witness double-digit percent rises in homicides last year. This implies that the virus cannot be the sole cause.

Officers were sometimes quarantined due to exposure or cases in their ranks, lowering the number of officers available for patrol, investigation, or protest coverage. Keeping a physical distance during protests was next to impossible.

2) The U.S. Protests over Police Brutality: Protests over black men and boys slain by police — Michael Brown in Ferguson, Tamir Rice in Cleveland, Freddie Gray in Baltimore, and others — swept through cities beginning in 2014, followed by an increase in murder and other violence. Several parties in the ensuing argument claimed a "Ferguson effect", despite the fact that there has been little empirical study to support this assertion.

One idea argued that cops backed off from proactive enforcement because they were fearful of being caught up in the next viral event that would lead to demonstrations. On the other hand, the public may have lost trust in police and may have been less willing to help as witnesses or informants, making it more difficult to conclude investigations, make arrests, and remove dangerous people from the streets.

A growing conviction that the criminal justice system cannot be trusted may also have prompted some to take matters into their hands violently.

In late May 2020, a video of George Floyd dying under the knee of a Minneapolis police officer went viral on social media, sparking one of the greatest protest movements in American history. Protest messages ranged from defunding departments to total elimination of police forces, and they were occasionally violent, leading to looting and other property destruction.

Many protesters questioned the legitimacy of American law enforcement. Police forces were frequently forced to relocate police from high-crime areas to downtown areas in order to staff rallies.

Sometimes protesters blocked major intersections and traffic, and the police had to man all those protests. They couldn't leave them unattended. So, they weren't able to be present in neighborhoods.

"It's not that the protests caused the increase in violence," said Peter Moskos, a former Baltimore police officer, and professor at John Jay College of Criminal Justice's Department of Law, Police Science, and Criminal Justice Administration. "The protests resulted in a significant shift in the police. When policing is reduced, violence rises."

As a result, the nationwide increase in violence can be linked to police forces that are "stretched to the breaking point" in dealing with protests and coronavirus restrictions.

3) America's Gun Problem: The United States possesses the most civilian guns, and the number of firearms purchased by Americans has increased dramatically in recent years. The science is clear: more firearms mean more gun violence and more lethal violence because the presence of a gun permits almost any confrontation to escalate, from public squabbles to domestic abuse. Even if fresh gun purchases aren't to blame, existing guns possibly are.

Last year, more persons carried guns, which led to more police officers discovering firearms during arrests. So it's possible that people did not buy more firearms as they began carrying the arsenal of weapons they already possessed.

Ironically, the U.S. doesn't track gun ownership or sales. While we know that U.S. residents bought weapons in unprecedented quantities last year, gun ownership data is incomplete at best. The FBI monitors pre-sale background checks, but there is no federal database of gun purchases, and there is no mechanism to account for guns obtained illegally.

According to an FBI report, about 40 million firearm background checks were performed last year, the most ever in a single year. According to the National Shooting Sports Foundation, 21 million of those background checks were exclusively related to gun transactions.

Allow that to sink in.

According to the Gun Violence Archive's data, approximately 20,000 individuals were killed by gun violence in the United States last year, and there were about 200 more mass shootings in 2020 than in 2019.

Unfortunately, certain people are more likely than others to be victims or perpetrators of gun violence. Violence breeds violence, and trauma breeds trauma. As a result of the economic troubles caused by the pandemic, people have recently been compelled to figure out how to survive and make ends meet.

Perhaps the best answer is that all of these elements were involved.

Regional Differences in Crime in the United States

The rate of violence and property crime varies greatly from state to state and city to city. Even within the same state, the crime rate can vary greatly amongst cities of similar size. The FBI emphasizes that a variety of factors, such as population density and economic conditions, might influence a region's crime rate.

According to Laura Cooper, executive director of the Major Cities Chiefs Association, a number of major cities still suffered a high rate of violent crime in the first three months of 2021. "Some cities are on track to outperform last year's figures," she said.

Murders increased by over 14 percent in **New York** City between March 20 and March 21, according to the most recent information released by the department, while gunshots increased by nearly 50 percent.

Homicides in **Los Angeles** climbed about 36% from 67 to 91 through March 30, according to LAPD Officer Rosario Cervantes.

In **Chicago**, homicides are up 33% in the first three months of the year compared to the same period in 2020, while gunshots are up nearly 40%.

The homicide increase in the three cities comes after **Chicago**, **Houston**, and **Memphis** experienced some of the highest increases in homicides last year, with an increase of 100 or more killings compared to 2019. A single day in Chicago saw

18 homicides, the highest total in the city's history. The pandemic had a particularly harsh impact on communities that had already suffered a higher number of shootings and homicides.

Baltimore, one of three jurisdictions in the MCCA report that did not report an increase in violent crime, likewise saw mainly peaceful protests without the kind of rioting and looting seen in other cities. According to Baltimore Police Commissioner Michael Harrison, the correlation between the spike in crime and the moving of police resources may be found here, particularly in cities that have seen large-scale protests over the period of several months. According to the Commissioner, a minor decrease in violent crime in Baltimore last year is "nothing to celebrate" because the city's stats are much higher than most, with 335 homicides last year compared to 348 in 2019.

According to Chuck Wexler, executive director of the Police Executive Research Forum (PERF), a national policy research and policy organization, Baltimore needed to work hard to recover public trust after the murder of Freddie Gray, a 25-year-old black man who died in police custody in 2015. According to Wexler, while there was turmoil in Baltimore in the early days of last summer's protest movement, it calmed down in ways that did not occur in other places such as Portland, Seattle, and New York.

According to the city's Commissioner, following protests in June 2020, killings in **St. Louis, Missouri** increased significantly. According to Commissioner Hayden of the St.

Louis Metropolitan Police Department, the city saw fewer homicides in June than in 2019, but the totals in June and July were significantly higher than in 2019. "It was homicide after homicide," Hayden explained.

That's just out of the ordinary for St. Louis. At the same time, due to the Covid pandemic, entire units were sometimes shut down. According to the Commissioner, for every officer or two sick, ten people may be quarantined. Because of illness and quarantine, the virus made it difficult for police to field fully staffed teams. You can't keep your distance when ordered to congregate for masked protests and civil disturbance, as it isn't possible to maintain safety regulations in these situations. Due to this fact, quarantines had a considerable impact on the ability to confront violent crime as well as protests to the extent that was required.

Worse yet, COVID-19 brought the criminal justice system to a halt. According to analysts, COVID-19 has had a significant impact on the criminal justice system sectors that hold offenders accountable for their actions. Jails, prisons, and correctional facilities were hotspots for COVID-19 infections among inmates and employees, causing some authorities to cut populations and suspend new detainee admissions drastically. Courts that were chronically overcrowded were obliged to close, postpone, or cancel hearings entirely. In order to restrict in-person interactions, state and municipal jury trials were severely constrained. Prosecutors had to change the way they pursued cases as well.

According to a report by the Johns Hopkins Bloomberg School of Public Health, the criminal justice system is "highly susceptible to the spread of COVID-19 due to the structure of carceral facilities, which propagates the spread of respiratory infections, and the comorbidities of many incarcerated individuals."

According to Baltimore's Commissioner Harrison, the elements that influence why an individual decides to commit a crime have everything to do with the chance of being caught, and if they are caught, whether there will be penalties. According to him, nearly a year-long shutdown of the criminal justice system communicated the message that people would not be held accountable for their crimes.

"When violent crime offenders are not held accountable by the criminal justice system, people are victimized again," said Cooper, the president of the Major Cities Chiefs Association. "If there is a mechanism to avoid further victimization, it must be implemented. Unfortunately, in many instances, this has not occurred."

The underlying issue is that people are concerned about their safety. The pandemic has changed the way individuals mourn the loss of a loved one, funerals have been restricted, and adult support groups have not met as frequently. People do not have a place to express their trauma. Thus, both COVID-19 and protests fueled a sense that the social fabric was fraying, and more people, particularly in the poorest areas, felt they had to fend for themselves. They armed themselves with guns so that they could act on their own if they felt threatened.

As a result, any particular conflict was more likely to escalate into lethal violence. Unfortunately, every act of violence has the potential to destroy a family, and we must not mistake people's perseverance and resolve to endure for tolerance or indifference. In the inner cities and areas where violence is pervasive, we are always dealing with trauma. Unfortunately, the damage is exacerbated in youngsters who are constantly exposed to violent crime from a young age.

Hence, it should be highlighted that whenever we discuss violent crime, we should do it from the victims' perspective. As a result, when we say there has been an increase, it also means that there has been an increase in the victimization of community members.

My Story

My name is Aubin Jack, and I am the founder, owner, and president of National Alert Security and Protection Services, Inc. (NASPS). I have over 20 years of military experience and over 15 years of hands-on business experience in the security field.

I work in the private security sector and possess a unique combination of experience and background in the army. I specialize in executive protection/bodyguards, armed and unarmed security, consulting, transportation, and provision of all sorts of security and training as well as equipment with the latest technology. I have dedicated my life to protecting people and keeping them safe.

NASPS is a fully licensed and certified armed and unarmed security and executive protection agency in Florida that primarily serves Miami-Dade, Broward, and Palm Beach counties. We are open to working and providing security in the United States and around the world, given the correct circumstances. We are committed to the safety and security of our customers, clients, and the community. Our staff and employees have vast experience in security as well as extensive service with governmental agencies, law enforcement, and military operations.

The necessity to defend individuals and property has always existed, but it has become essential as the country's threat level rises, resulting in the rapid growth of the private security business. I've noticed a marginal increase in domestic issues in the last several years, and then Covid struck, people's social safety nets vanished, and things swiftly deteriorated.

So far, an increasingly dangerous situation has emerged. Shockingly in recent times, I have had to respond to 21 domestic violence situations during my line of work since 2020. Thus, in such trying times, the typical security guard approach of deterrence is insufficient to safeguard individuals or families. More emphasis needs to be placed on developing preventative and protection measures rather than the more traditional approach.

Furthermore, because security is not a core competency for most businesses, outsourcing is frequently more efficient, and as crime increases, large players are likely to join the security industry with more staff to keep up, as the need for crime prevention and detection increases. This indicates that more people must be trained in how to handle these types of situations and threats. That is what prompted me to write this book.

The Book's Purpose

Security professionals may be unable to reform, enlighten, or civilize a culture to the heinous reality of crime and abuse. However, we can and must do the dual role of advocates and activists to protect those at risk. Our world is filled with both external and internal threats. Since Covid, there has been a considerable increase in domestic and gun violence in the USA.

This book aims to alert victims living in an abusive environment to confront this threat now at the disturbance level before the violence escalates and call 911 to remove the threat from your home and at the hands of the police if you are currently being abused. This publication is also a platform to inform security professionals that old security methods aren't effective to safeguard individuals, families, and communities against domestic and gun violence.

It endeavors to provide practical assistance and extensive explanation of the private security professional's roles and obligations. It can serve as a great on-the-job reference, training manual, and teaching resource. Finally, this book addresses the need for citizens in neighborhoods to work together and confront the current threats of domestic and gun violence at the grass roots level.

The private security sector is an important part of security and safety in the United States and around the world. Today, private security is in charge of safeguarding many of the nation's institutions, vital infrastructure systems, intellectual property, and sensitive corporate data. This is in addition to shielding its individuals, society, and organizations from ordinary criminality and law violations.

Its significance to our criminal justice system and our nation's safety and security necessitates that we review and revise the practices and guidelines of the private security industry. It is critical to stay current in the business, grow, and learn new skills and best practices. In addition, discover effective strategies for crisis management, asset protection, and other protection techniques.

Chapter 2: What Is Security

Security is defined in a variety of ways in Webster's dictionary, such as freedom from danger, anxiety, or the prospect of being laid off. Another definition of security is what secures or protects, such as measures intended to prevent espionage or sabotage, crime, attack, or escape, in an organization or department. For security professionals, the term "security" is directly connected with efforts to keep persons, individuals, and groups safe from danger.

Thus, security is a method, and being safe is the finished result. Products offer some safety, but the only way to do business effectively in an unsafe world is to implement procedures and engage with professionals who acknowledge the environment's underlying insecurity.

However, the pandemic caused the roles of a security professional to change dramatically. Many security professionals were required to update emergency preparedness plans, conduct risk assessments, and manage health-related concerns and procedures in response to the COVID-19 epidemic, social and civic upheaval, the election, and other factors. This past year, security departments have widened their reach to better grasp new needs and threats confronting individuals and businesses and how to adapt to a highly reactive environment. Aided with the advancement of technology, security has taken on new meaning, with some parts being social media-driven threats, bullying, and intimidation rather than actual physical threats.

Violence Is Spiking

Crime rates in the United States are currently at an all-time high[9]. Approximately 70 million firearms were sold in the month preceding the election.[10] To suggest that the United States is an armed camp would be an understatement. This has contributed to the issues that we face on a daily basis in every security area.

In the case of healthcare, to assist in maintaining a helpful and secure work environment, it is critical that we now incorporate security, safety, preventive, and de-escalation into the very fabric of every member of the medical management.

Recently, the Justice Department announced the commencement of a five-city initiative in the United States to combat rising gun violence by targeting illegal gun trafficking and pursuing charges that aid in the acquisition of firearms by criminals.[11] On the other hand, violent crimes, including homicides and shootings, are on the rise in many places around the country. The Biden administration has promised to assist communities plagued by violence.

There are two ideas to explain this increase: one is that police are withdrawing because they are irritated by the antagonism they meet in the community, and the other is that communities

---

[9] Horton, B. J. (2021, July 7). *US crime: Is America seeing a surge in violence?* BBC News. https://www.bbc.com/news/57581270

[10] Stephen, S. (2021, April 22). *Gun sales hit all-time high amid flurry of mass shootings.* CBS News. https://www.cbsnews.com/news/gun-sales-on-pace-to-hit-new-record-in-2021/

[11] Balsamo, M. (2021, July 22). *Garland launches new effort to curb gun trafficking in US cities.* The Christian Science Monitor. https://www.csmonitor.com/USA/Justice/2021/0722/Garland-launches-new-effort-to-curb-gun-trafficking-in-US-cities

that no longer trust police are taking vigilante justice into their hands.

Here are some recent statistics for you:

In 2020, Denver and Aurora saw a significant increase in homicides, and far too many people have been grieving. In the first six months of 2021, thirteen people were killed in homicides in Aurora, and 74 others were shot but managed to survive. That is on track to match the levels of gun violence seen in 2020 when gun violence increased, and the number of homicides and shootings more than doubled from the previous year.[12] More people have been injured in shootings in the first half of 2021 than in all of 2019.

Domestic violence stats are not pleasing either, increasing at unprecedented rates since 2020 in the United States.[13]

This means the country's law and order situation demands that its citizens take personal measures to ensure their safety. With crimes rising and more and more guns purchased every day, it is difficult for the average American to keep themselves safe. Not everybody has a thing for guns, nor the attitude to confront dangerous situations. This is where security agencies come into play.

---

[12] Schmelzer, E. (2021, July 20). *"There isn't a Band-Aid": Gun violence in Aurora continues at alarming level, police chief says.* The Denver Post. https://www.denverpost.com/2021/07/19/aurora-crime-gun-violence-2021/

[13] *Access Restricted.* (n.d.). Kxan. Retrieved August 31, 2021, from https://www.kxan.com/news/covid-19-isolation-causing-rise-in-domestic-violence-in-texas-across-country/

Facilities and Services of Security Agencies

The tasks of a security officer might range from merely being a presence to responding to robberies and assaults and maintaining law and order. Knowing all of the duties of a security officer goes a long way toward assuring the safety of your property. Their work description includes a variety of duties and obligations, such as inspecting and patrolling the premises on a regular basis, monitoring property entrance, authorizing the entrance of individuals and vehicles, reporting any suspicious behaviors and happenings, and so on. As well as keeping an eye on the surveillance cameras, responding to alarms and acting quickly, and providing support to those in need.

They are primarily responsible for maintaining law and order on the site. In the event of an emergency, the officer should control the situation and keep order as best as they can. They should also be able to communicate effectively and lead decisively while waiting for authorities to arrive on the site. This is popular in office/corporate security, residential security, and hotel security.

This task is frequently a balancing act. While the security officers are assisting guests, they must simultaneously be aware of their other obligations, such as recognizing potential threats and restricting entry to potentially dangerous people.

It can be said that the function of the police is diminishing, or they are not performing their duties properly. Otherwise, people wouldn't have turned to security agencies. Anecdotal evidence shows it can take over seven minutes for law enforcement to arrive at a 911 scene in a lot of cities. Seven minutes is a lot of time. Anything can happen in seven minutes, let alone within minutes.

What Is a Security Officer?

Private security guards have outnumbered police officers since the 1980s,[14] but the increased concern about security following the September 11, 2001 attacks has resulted in an estimated one million contract security officers and an equivalent number of guards working directly for U.S. firms. This is significantly more than the approximately 700,000 sworn law enforcement officials in the United States.[15]

The number of licensed security officers and guards in the USA is remarkable. However, only a small number of guards have the motivation and dedication to become officers. Security officers are professionals in this field and are capable of making rational independent decisions while executing higher levels of responsibilities. They are dedicated to mission accomplishment, motivated at work, and constantly driven to improve themselves, the individuals, and the communities they serve. They are the people I seek for executive protection services and I help provide long-term training plans for. The four key components of this training plan are:

---

[14] *JSTOR: Access Check.* (n.d.-b). JSTOR. Retrieved August 31, 2021, from http://www.jstor.org/stable/800267

[15] Statista. (2021, February 2). *Number of law enforcement officers U.S. 2004–2019.* https://www.statista.com/statistics/191694/number-of-law-enforcement-officers-in-the-us/

Physical Fitness

Some people simply talk the talk while others walk the talk. This profession requires you to walk the talk. Security professionals cannot protect themselves or their clients from threats if they aren't fit. This becomes more apparent as you get older. Therefore, I believe that fitness is essential in this line of work. You may have to walk, run, pull, lift, carry, drag, push, or strike, all the while staying vigilant.

If the threat is imminent, security officers must be able to move the client quickly to a safe and secure location or engage the threat. So it's absolutely critical for them to be in shape and to be continually working on improving their fitness. The four key components of physical wellness that all security professionals must train to improve are:

1. **Endurance:** This is the most fundamental part of physical fitness. Security professionals must have the stamina to endure long, unpleasant, or difficult situations. They must be able to exert themselves and remain active and alert for longer periods of time. They must also be able to resist, withstand, or quickly recover from trauma, wounds, and fatigue as they will come across many high-stress situations.

2. **Strength:** Strength training makes your bones stronger, lowers your risk of injury, and can boost your self-esteem. It can help to improve your joint's range of motion and improve brain health. It is also integral to self-defense and fighting tactics, which can be required at any point in time during the security officer's duty.

3. **Balance:** Balance training is often neglected but it is a crucial part of any fitness training. Security officers are required to walk long distances, go up and down stairs, and run. Therefore, incorporating balance training in your fitness plan will help to improve coordination, joint stability, and long-term health.

4. **Flexibility:** Flexibility training helps to improve physical activity by lengthening and stretching the muscles to prevent injury. Additionally, it helps to reduce muscle stiffness by helping your joints move through their full range of motion. This will help improve posture while helping to reduce aches and pains.

Mental Intelligence

Security professionals must have a hunger to learn the art of this profession. They should seek higher education, read and study professional materials, and constantly work to improve their problem-solving abilities. Therefore, critical thinking and situational awareness are essential in this line of work because security officers will be required to make smart and quick decisions to mitigate threats.

The security officer must have an above-average understanding of tech, machinery, and computers, and must be trained in areas like first aid, patrolling, situational awareness, CPR, etc. Training to learn new strategies and techniques is continuous and required in order to do the job more efficiently.

Emotional Intelligence

Security professionals must develop the ability to manage and use their emotions in a positive manner to verbally diffuse conflicts and handle difficult situations. We use Daniel Goleman's five elements as guidelines for emotional intelligence training:[16]

1. **Self-Awareness:** This is the ability to recognize and understand your emotions and feelings. This is a critical emotional intelligence skill as it allows you to be aware of your moods and actions and what effect they have on other people. It can help one recognize their strengths and limitations and also help them improve with new information and experiences. Self-aware people know what is best for them and what to do to become the best versions of themselves. They are confident and easy-going and also learn quickly. They are aware of their abilities and how other people perceive them and can manipulate them to the best of their advantage. Self-awareness also gives way to a greater understanding of other individuals and their way of thinking since the human psyche works more or less in the same way for everyone.

2. **Self-Regulation:** In addition to being aware of your emotions and feelings, it is important to know how to respond to them properly. This includes being able to manage and regulate your emotions in order to elicit the best response in any given circumstance. This is a key part of your emotional

---

[16] Cherry, K. C. (2021, January 13). 5 Key Emotional Intelligence Skills. Very Well Mind. https://www.verywellmind.com/components-of-emotional-intelligence-2795438

intelligence as it allows you to practice the insight you gain via self-awareness to achieve the best version of yourself. Self-regulation is important in this field of work since difficult and tense situations can test your patience. A security officer is always required to maintain a calm and composed demeanor, no matter what the conditions are. It would be difficult if a guard had no self-regulatory mechanism and lost control of their emotions during a conflict. This would only make things worse for the client. People with strong self-regulation skills are thoughtful about the way they influence others, and they are always ready to take responsibility for their actions. They're good at managing conflict and are able to diffuse tense and difficult situations effectively. They are also flexible and tend to adapt well to change. As I mentioned before, all of these qualities are required of a security officer who is working in this business.

3.   **Motivation:** Motivation is another key factor that pushes forward into the emotional intelligence of a person. The security officer must always have their eyes set on the goal and must fulfill their duties without ever straying too far from the intended task. This is why they must have the intrinsic motivation or an internal drive that keeps them moving forward with their duty to protect the client. According to Daniel, emotionally intelligent people are motivated by things that are beyond temporary and superficial rewards like fame, money, and recognition. Their drive comes from wanting to fulfill their duty to the best of their experience and from an integral sense of right and wrong. People with a good intrinsic drive have a well-aligned moral compass and are completely in tune with all

of their activities. They work to the best of their abilities and almost never disappoint in fulfilling a task. They are competent and action-oriented and do their jobs with utmost commitment.

4. **Social Skills:** Being able to interact well with others is another aspect of emotional intelligence that is important in this business and in all fields of work. Strong social skills allow people to develop deep professional relationships with their clients, which then allow for a greater understanding of the task at hand. Some important social skills that are absolutely essential for each security officer to possess are good verbal communication skills, the ability to understand and interpret non-verbal cues, leadership skills, persuasiveness, and active listening.

5. **Empathy:** Empathy entails recognizing and understanding how others are feeling and what is their current emotional status. As much as it's important to be able to recognize your own emotions, it is also just as important to be able to understand what another person is going through. Empathy can be the driving force that can motivate a security officer to do his job in the best possible way. Knowing what their client is going through can help them connect with their client on a deeper level and encourage them to make sure their client is safe. Being able to identify a certain mood or recognize the emotional atmosphere can also be helpful in deciding how to respond to a certain situation. Being empathetic can give you the ability to understand the power dynamics that occur, which eventually influence interpersonal relationships.

Ethical Intelligence

Clients expect security officers to be honest, trustworthy, and to do the right thing all the time. They expect security officers to be consummate professionals with exemplary character. Therefore, ethical intelligence encompasses the ability to make moral decisions when faced with integrity challenges. This is something that many people don't address, but it is crucial especially in a crisis situation.

Veterans Are the Key

Veterans are a key resource for security agencies and can be immediately placed into executive protection and other protection types of details. They have proven themselves by serving their country honorably and can now serve in communities where their expertise is needed.

Security is unquestionably a job industry that draws a large number of veterans. This is why organizations typically recruit ex-military for practically every major security venue. A veteran's knowledge of laws, regulations, weaponry, and authority will come in handy in this industry. While digital alarms, cameras, and other non-human technology can improve security, there is no substitute for a trained individual. As a result, veterans can continue to serve their country and be a significant asset in the security industry.

Security threats have undoubtedly evolved. Domestic terrorism and extremist groups have become a substantial menace in recent years. As a result, the demand for professional, qualified, and licensed security service professionals has increased, which will go a long way toward ensuring that all responsibilities are carried out with the vigilance that they should be.

The next generation of security professionals will need more specialized skills, tools, and expertise than previous generations. These individuals must train and update themselves in accordance with the environment and job requirements.

Chapter 3: COVID-19

On March 11, 2020, the World Health Organization declared the COVID-19 outbreak a pandemic and, based on its prior assessment of the threat posed by this virus, relayed public health measures that brought our lives to a near halt. The situation escalated pretty quickly, with borders being shut down with travel bans to schools and workplaces being sealed.

A global lockdown was set into place with public restrictions and the issuance of nationwide stay-at-home orders. You could see it launch a wave of fear as the pain, death, and suffering took the whole world by storm. Hospitals were overwhelmed by the relentless influx of COVID-19 patients, and people were confused and frustrated as they lost their loved ones.

One thing that particularly came as a shock was that America was one of the countries where the impact of the virus was seen to be the most profound. By the end of 2020, the death toll in America was almost 375,000 - the highest figure in the whole world, with about 3000 people dying every day. About one-fifth of the confirmed global coronavirus deaths were from the United States.[17]

The virus not only compromised the mental and physical well-being of the local public, but it also affected their livelihood. With the economic state on an all-time low since the Great Depression, a great range of businesses and industrial sectors were impacted by the outbreak, although not all of them

---

[17] Hills, M. H. (2020, December 12). Covid-19 in the US: Bleak winter ahead as deaths surge. BBC News. https://www.bbc.com/news/world-us-canada-54966531

were impacted equally. The economic crisis originated in both, the supply and demand sectors. With social restrictions leading to a total or partial suspension of social and productive activities, sectors whose activities involved physical proximity and social interactions like tourism, hotels, outdoor entertainment, restaurants, and transport took a greater hit compared to sectors that were deemed essential like food, cleaning supplies, and pharmaceuticals. An interruption in productive activities like trade and travel restrictions also generated problems with supply chains, both domestic and imported, even for the companies that continue to operate.

There has been a significant change in the consumption patterns with the shift in consumer priorities. Also, I believe there has been a drop in consumption due to reduced consumer incomes, courtesy of COVID-19. This has negatively affected consumer durables segments like furniture, household appliances, cars, clothing, and footwear, while goods and services like disinfectant products, canned foods, telecommunications, and internet and television services have flourished. Many aspects of the international situation, such as the abrupt fall in oil prices, have generated a widespread drop in returns on export and external demands.

The manufacturing sector has overall suffered as well, especially the technology-intensive and labor-intensive industries. Various industries with the highest technological content are facing a severe crisis. These branches are the ones that bring together the most learning and innovation-intensive activities that are fundamental in order to close productivity gaps. This situation may therefore deepen the already existing structural problems of our economy.

The sectors that Covid has negatively impacted are a source of over a third of formal employment accounts for about a quarter of the total Gross Domestic Product. This has only contributed to making the current situation even more unpredictable.[18]

The International Labor Organization (ILO) conducted some preliminary assessments of the impact of COVID-19 on certain social and economic sectors and devised policy responses in order to prevent further crisis. Let's look at the sector-wise response of each business in the course of this pandemic.[19]

Impact on the Education Sector

Schools and universities closed at the start of the pandemic in an attempt to lower the spread of coronavirus. This shutdown interrupted learning for about 1.58 billion learners around the world[20]. However, this allowed education systems to employ transformative strategies of using technology-based alternatives to traditional classroom settings. School systems are now using more online teaching methods such as

---

[18] United Nations. (2020). Sectors and businesses facing COVID-19: Emergency and reactivation. United Nation ECLAC, 3–5. https://repositorio.cepal.org/bitstream/handle/11362/45736/5/S2000437_en.pdf

[19] International Labour Organization. (n.d.). Sectoral impact, responses and recommendations. Retrieved August 31, 2021, from https://www.ilo.org/global/topics/coronavirus/sectoral/lang--en/index.htm

[20] *Check out this UNESCO's Futures of education IDEAS LAB post: Sustaining learning communities through and beyond COVID-19.* (n.d.). UNESCO. Retrieved August 31, 2021, from https://en.unesco.org/futuresofeducation/holmes-sustaining-learning-communities-COVID-19

videoconferencing and sharing learning material through messaging platforms and school-based intranets. However, this virtual learning is only said to exacerbate existing inequalities in education by limiting the spread of knowledge only to those who can afford to have technological resources like a good device and an internet connection. It has also created frustrations among the young who are not meeting and physically socializing with their peers.

Impact on the Tourism Sector

This industry has been hit hard by the pandemic with the necessary measures that were taken to control the virus. Travel restrictions had a devastating impact on all tourism enterprises that had no way to earn once the stay-at-home orders came through.

[21]In 2019, the tourism sector accounted for about 330 million jobs worldwide, directly or indirectly. This is equivalent to 10.3% of the total global employment, so you can well assume how massive the impact of the pandemic would have been on this sector. Statistics show that the efforts to contain the virus will effectively contract the international tourism economy by 45% to 70%.[22]

---

[21] *Travel & Tourism Economic Impact | World Travel & Tourism Council (WTTC)*. (n.d.). WTTC. Retrieved August 31, 2021, from https://wttc.org/Research/Economic-Impact
[22] International Labour Organization. (2020, May). The impact of COVID-19 on the tourism sector. ILO. https://www.ilo.org/wcmsp5/groups/public/---ed_dialogue/---sector/documents/briefingnote/wcms_741468.pdf

Impact on the Health Sector

With the health sector being on the front lines of this pandemic, it has been substantially affected in the past year and a half. [23]By January 31st, 2021, health workers accounted for up to 1.29 million COVID-19 cases, which is roughly 8% of the total cases.

Not only this, but healthcare workers also have to serve longer working hours due to a severe shortage in the workforce.[24] Hospitals are also facing a shortage of medical equipment with a growing number of patients and people requiring medical aid. It has also led to income losses among health system actors who are not front-line workers and specialize in other fields since everybody is avoiding the hospital except for emergencies.

Impact on Food Retail

In times like these, people look for security, and so food retails and grocery stores are important. However, social distancing restrictions have prompted more and more people to conduct their transactions and grocery shopping online. Since the start of the lockdown, crowd traffic at fast food and casual dining restaurants has decreased by 49% and 61% respectively.[25] Many stores, therefore, have been closed down,

---

[23] *devex.com.* (n.d.-b). Devex. Retrieved August 31, 2021, from https://www.devex.com/news/covid-19-a-timeline-of-the-coronavirus-outbreak-96396

[24] International Labour Organization. (2020a, April). COVID-19 and the health sector. ILO. https://www.ilo.org/wcmsp5/groups/public/---ed_dialogue/---sector/documents/briefingnote/wcms_741655.pdf

[25] The impact of COVID-19 on eating, restaurants and fast-food chains. (n.d.). Better Connected Marketing. Retrieved August 31, 2021, from

and restaurants have been on a systemic loss since the start. Fast food and grocery delivery services, however, are flourishing more and more by the day. Food delivery has been up by almost 12% on weekdays, while there has been a comparative decrease in orders on the weekend since 'weekends' have essentially lost their meaning. The bigger supermarket chains and food retails are now facing a shortage of employees. There has been increased recruitment of employees both in warehouses and food stores to satisfy online deliveries and work at checkout counters.

Walmart declared that it was planning to recruit over 150,000 hourly workers for its stores, while Instacart, a grocery delivery service, declared that it was planning to recruit more than 300,000 workers.[26] These facilities have mostly been afforded by large retailers, while smaller food retail businesses have had no other option but to shut down since they cannot afford such e-commerce tactics.

Impact on Textiles, Clothing, Leather, and Footwear Industries

Since garments and accessories are considered secondary to survival, people have mostly avoided spending their money on them. Especially due to the uncertain financial situations of a major part of the population, it has suppressed consumer demand by a great deal. Also, the closure of retail stores has only

---

https://www.wearemiq.com/blog/the-impact-of-covid-19-on-eating-restaurants-and-fast-food-chains/

[26] International Labour Organization. (2020, June). COVID-19 and food retail. ILO. https://www.ilo.org/wcmsp5/groups/public/---ed_dialogue/---sector/documents/briefingnote/wcms_741342.pdf

reinforced the disparities in this sector. There has been a sharp drop in textile sales, and many people have been laid off as a result. Let me give you some statistics from around the world so you can consider the United State in the larger global context. In Cambodia, an estimated 200 factories have either been suspended or have reduced production, which has led to about 5,000 people losing their jobs. A lack of raw material from China has led to the closure of about 20 factories in Myanmar and the loss of 10,000 jobs. In Vietnam, about 440,000 to 880,000 workers are estimated to be at risk of reduced hours or unemployment, and in Bangladesh, at least 2.17 million workers have been affected, with many facing unemployment.

Similarly, apparel and footwear organizations in the U.S. have suffered. They have asked for temporary tariff relief so that they can ensure the payment of salaries of about four million workers who had been affected. Even major brands like Adidas, H&M, Gap, and Inditex have experienced dwindling stock prices.[27]

The Impact of COVID-19 on Security Companies

It was seen that most of the businesses that were directly associated with security had the worst impact. Hotels, events, churches, state and local governments, restaurants, airlines, tourism, theme parks, banks, gym, and schools, all these different areas directly affected security. They were sealed,

---

[27] International Labour Organization. (2020b, April). COVID-19 and the textiles, clothing, leather and footwear industries. ILO. https://www.ilo.org/wcmsp5/groups/public/---ed_dialogue/---sector/documents/briefingnote/wcms_741344.pdf

started operating at minimum manning, and no longer needed security individuals for their safekeeping.

It especially became a major problem when many of these businesses were permanently shut down due to their losses. On September 28, 2020, Fortune Magazine stated that 97,996 businesses had shut down.[28] On May 16, 2021, the Wall Street Journal came out with 200,000 additional closures that were taking place.

NBC News stated that many closures weren't temporary. As per the NBC news report, 60% of these closures were permanent as of April 2021.[29] This situation directly correlated with what was happening in the security business.

Many businesses started thinking ahead. While some organizations had to shut their doors due to the lockdown, others started to conduct business activities from home. That's when the sources hypothesized that domestic violence rates would start to go up as a result of this house confinement, but they had no idea that there would be a spike like this.

People were spending more time with their families, and many of these family situations were not really ideal. People were stressed about many things. They were stressed about the

[28] Sraders, A. S., & Lambert, L. L. (2020, August 28). Nearly 100,000 establishments that temporarily shut down due to the pandemic are now out of business. Fortune. https://fortune.com/2020/09/28/covid-buisnesses-shut-down-closed/
[29] Sundaram, A. S. (202–09-16). Almost 60 percent of business closures are now permanent, new Yelp data shows. NBC News. https://www.nbcnews.com/business/economy/almost-60-percent-business-closures-are-now-permanent-new-yelp-n1240209

uncertainty of paying rent, they're going to pay their bills, and the uncertainty of their health.

Schools, colleges, and universities were shut down as people were suffering from financial insecurities. Children were not able to go out and play, and parents had to work from home. They were all together in the same house, which created stressful situations that allowed domestic violence to rise more than anyone had envisioned.

Conclusion

Security companies should look at shifting some of their forces to help make a difference against domestic violence. Before the pandemic, workplace violence in itself was an area that required some assistance from security agencies. Now that many people are working from home, it's posing a greater threat disguised as domestic violence. It is as Kakuzo Okakaura says,

"The art of life is a constant readjustment to our surroundings."

Chapter 4: Domestic Violence

Domestic violence is defined by the Centers for Disease Control and Prevention as "physical violence, sexual violence, stalking, and psychological aggression (including coercive acts) by a current or former intimate partner". With COVID-19 on the rise and the recent quarantine conditions, there has been a sharp increase in domestic violence around the United States.

There has been a 30% spike in domestic violence cases since the start of the pandemic. The numbers have kept rising since then. Even now that the COVID-19 conditions have settled a bit, domestic violence rates are still on a high. Many things have come up out of this, including instances of physical abuse, emotional abuse, divorces, and drug abuse. And it all seems to be stemming right from the catastrophe, which was the pandemic.

Victims of domestic violence mainly included intimate partner and child abuse, which were at significant risk of sustaining severe injuries, including death. It is an alarming situation to know that domestic violence increased by 8.1% during the COVID-19 pandemic. According to National Commission on COVID-19 and Criminal Justice (NCCCJ), the rise in domestic violence is due to economic stress and lockdowns caused during the COVID-19 pandemic. Initial domestic violence reports during the COVID-19 pandemic phase were based on police reports. However, with careful analysis by the NCCCJ, the data from the police call logs, domestic violence reports, emergency and medical records show overwhelming evidence of an increase in domestic violence.[30] A Women's Aid report in the United Kingdom found that 61% of the women living with their abusers said that their abuse had worsened during the lockdown. Massachusetts hospital recognized a significant annual jump in intimate partner violence cases who sought emergency care during the pandemic's first week, with nearly all the victims being women. According to the data collected by Legal Templates, from March to June 2020, the number of people looking into divorce was 34% higher than those same months in 2019. The interest in separation also peaked on April 13th, 2020, just two to three weeks after the lockdown was imposed in many states.[31]

The ten states with the highest rates of domestic violence are:[32]

- Oklahoma (49.10%)

- Iowa (45.30%)

- Kentucky (45.30%)

- North Carolina (43.90%)

- Nevada (43.80%)

- Alaska (43.30%)

---

[30] Leah Rodriguez, (2021, March 3) Domestic Violence Increased in the U.S. by 8.1% During the COVID-19 Pandemic

[31] Francis, S. (2020, October 30). *Op-ed: Uptick in domestic violence amid Covid-19 isolation.* CNBC. https://www.cnbc.com/2020/10/30/uptick-in-domestic-violence-amid-covid-19-isolation.html

[32] *Domestic Violence By State 2021.* (n.d.). WorldPopulation. Retrieved September 8, 2021, from https://worldpopulationreview.com/state-rankings/domestic-violence-by-state

- Arizona (42.60%)
- Washington (42.60%)
- Idaho (42.50%)
- Missouri (41.70%)

So Why Is This Happening?

While some people stay at home to be safe during the epidemic, survivors of domestic abuse may become stuck in violent situations. The pandemic has made it increasingly difficult for survivors to get the support they require because survivors were living in close quarters with their abusers. Another worrying trend is the severity of the abuse. In a pandemic situation, where many things are uncertain, and there is much isolation, the abuse might worsen. In conditions of greater uncertainty and stress, people tend to become more frustrated, which results in taking that frustration out on the ones closest to them. This is the leading factor of abuse within homes, and in the case of this pandemic, the quarantine period has only made it far worse.

Increase in Stress

With the pandemic, there has been a sudden surge in stress and anxiety levels among people since they are under constant fear of their social and financial security, their health, and their survival. With schools and daycares closed, there has also been an increased load on parents to partake in childcare than under normal circumstances. Along with that, they also had their workload to manage alongside all the other activities at home. It has put a lot of families in a dire situation. The kids had to stay at home for the entire year, completely isolated from the outside world. This had its effects on their mental development since they missed out on their crucial years of learning with only access to the internet that had been connecting them with other people. Along with that, some parents really relied on schools as it allowed them some freedom of movement, whether for their career or their social life. But with the pandemic, these systems changed overnight. Many people have had to relocate, and many people have had their family members fall sick because of the virus, which has also taken a toll on their mental well-being. Even in spite of the domestic violence spurge, they showed a unique group that stood out higher than any of the other domestic violence categories - intimate partner violence. That's even 30% higher than that of the next category.

The Isolation

It is true that man is a social animal, and under the current circumstances, they have had to retract behind and adapt to a lifestyle of quarantine and social isolation. This has also taken a great toll on the mental well-being of people. People have had lesser opportunities to see their friends, acquaintances, and even strangers. In cases of existing domestic abuse and in cases of dysfunctional families, this has only had a very destructive impact. People have not been able to reach their support groups, and there has been a decline in client numbers for domestic violence programs and shelters. People have refrained from approaching these institutions due to the constant fear of acquiring the virus. Trauma experts have warned that this could lead to even more abuse and an increase in suicide rates, self-harm, alcoholism, substance abuse, and various mental health issues. Familial and marital relationships are deteriorating behind closed doors. Social places like schools, grocery stores, offices, and workplaces have always been opportunities of respites for survivors of domestic violence. With their closure, these victims have been under constant and unrelenting threat. This effect is bound to take a toll on their mental health.

Families were put under a lot of stress. The family members who used to have outlets or the people they used to connect with in regard to some of these problems were left to deal with the situation on their own. Teenage kids who suffered from domestic abuse used to view school days as a relief. People with family issues often went out to escape their reality, but now, they had nowhere to go and were stuck with being at home with the people that stressed them out. According to the Washington Post, in Washington D.C., the number of calls to hotlines from domestic abuse victims has increased significantly, with the non-profit organization, D.C. Safe, receiving more than 1,500 calls since March 8. Domestic violence shelters in Connecticut have also seen an increase in the number of calls from people who are afraid that they'd be stuck inside with their abusive partners because of the outbreak.[33]

---

[33] Dzhanova, Y. (2020, April 1). *NY domestic violence programs see client numbers decline as coronavirus traps survivors at home.* CNBC.
https://www.cnbc.com/2020/03/31/new-york-coronavirus-domestic-violence-programs-see-decline-as-disease-spreads.html

The Economic Uncertainty

Financial insecurity has been at its peak since the start of the outbreak. There have been nearly seven million people who have been left jobless since the start of the pandemic. Out of the temporary closures in 2020, almost 98,000 businesses had been permanently shut down, and by May 2021, an additional 168,000 were permanently closed, which not only put more of a strain on families but also left them in an ultimate financial crisis. People have been constantly under the threat of homelessness due to the inability to pay rent, and it has likely been a major cause of stress.

Additionally, economic uncertainty has led to an increase in depression, alcohol abuse, violence, and shootings. It's not only domestic violence, but the social and financial instability of a majority of the population has given rise to a variety of other types of crimes. It has completely compromised the security of the majority of the people living in America. How has this impacted security? Well, at first, the majority of our calls were for hotels, banks, events, etc. The objective was primarily to deter threats. Now, the majority of my calls are associated with the threat, "We have a situation and we would like to hire you for bodyguard services." or "I need protection against my husband." Each situation may be different but the underlying factors associated with domestic violence are the same.

Chapter 5: The Basics

In the English Dictionary, the definition of abuse is given as an action that is carried out to harm someone or an action that is morally wrong, whether it be intentional or unintentional. Abuse is often carried out to gain benefit over someone else unfairly or dishonestly. Many different types of abuse exist, some of which can also be classified as criminal offenses. It can sometimes be quite hard to identify abuse and know when it is being carried out, which is why it is important to learn how to recognize any possible indicators that there might be. To do that, we must first understand all the different forms of abuse.

Physical Abuse

As its name indicates, physical abuse is an intentional act or behavior that harms another person by way of bodily contact, causing injury, trauma, or any other kind of physical or mental suffering. Both children and adults can find themselves becoming victims of physical abuse. It is one of the most common forms of maltreatment for children and is often done by a parent, caregiver, or an older sibling.

In adults, the victims are often women who are subject to their intimate partners' abuse. Physical abuse may involve hitting, slapping, kicking, punching, assault, hair-pulling, biting, scratching, pushing, scalding, burning, unlawful use of restraint, forced isolation or confinement, forced feeding, or withheld meals.

For people in relationships, physical abuse can start gradually, often with a small push or a slap, and then it progressively becomes worse over time. According to National Statistics, on average, about 20 people per minute are physically abused by their intimate partner in the United States. Nearly one in three women and one in four men have experienced some form of physical violence in their relationships.[34]

Indicators for this kind of abuse can be:

- Unexplained and frequent injuries like bruises, cuts, red marks, welts, muscle sprains, dislocated joints, or hair loss in clumps

- Changed or subdued behavior in the presence of a specific person

- Signs of malnourishment

- Signs of self-treated injuries

- Patterns of hospitalization for similar injuries

- Withdrawal from social activities

- Failing to seek medical treatment or making frequent visits to different Emergency Rooms so as not to raise suspicion.

Sexual Abuse

Sexual abuse is forcing unwanted or undesired sexual behavior onto someone else. It is when the offenders use force or

---

[34] NATIONAL STATISTICS. (n.d.). NCADV. Retrieved September 21, 2021, from https://ncadv.org/STATISTICS

take advantage of the victim's inability to give consent. Sexual abuse can include sexual bullying, sexual misconduct, rape, serial rape, sodomy, incest, and sexual slavery.

Statistics show that about one in three women falls victim to sexual abuse during their lifetime.[35] There are many things that come within the umbrella of sexual misconduct, including:

- Any indecent act performed to cause humiliation, stimulation, or sexual satisfaction

- Inappropriate touch anywhere on the body

- Repeated sexual propositions even when the person has previously demonstrated that they are not interested

- Non-consensual masturbation of either or both persons

- Degrading remarks about a person's sex or sexuality, including their sexual orientation

- Publicizing an inappropriate picture, video, or recording of someone without their consent for the purpose of humiliating or degrading the person

- Non-consensual sexual penetration or attempted penetration of the vagina, anus, or mouth

- Forced witnessing of sexual acts and any indecent exposure to pornography

---

[35] National Coalition Against Domestic Violence. (n.d.-a). If you need help: Call The National Domestic Violence Hotline 1–800-799-SAFE (7233) Or, online go to TheHotline.org Suggested citation: National Coalition Against Domestic Violence (2017). Domestic violence and sexual assault. Retrieved from http://ncadv.org/files/Domestic%20Violence%20and%20Sexual%20Abuse%20NCAD V.pdf. Domestic Violence & Sexual Assault. NCADV. Retrieved September 21, 2021, from https://assets.speakcdn.com/assets/2497/sexual_assault_dv.pdf

- Emotional manipulation into giving consent

- Sexual propositions even when the offender is aware that the person is not interested but wants to exploit a working relationship, dependency, or other services

Indicators of sexual abuse are:

- Bruising, especially on the thighs, buttocks, upper arms, and marks on the neck

- Unusual difficulty in walking or sitting

- Torn, stained, or bloody undergarments

- Unexplained infections, genital discharge, or sexually transmitted diseases

- Bleeding, pain, or itching in the genital or rectal area

- Signs of self-harm

- Incontinence unrelated to medical diagnosis

- Fear of touch or excessive apprehension

- Reluctance to be alone with a specific person

- Changed or subdued behavior

- Disturbances in sleep, poor concentration, and withdrawal from social activities

- Pregnancy in a woman who is unable to consent to intercourse

- Unexpected use of explicit language and changes in sexual behavior

Psychological Abuse or Emotional Abuse

Psychological or emotional abuse is a kind of abuse where the assailant's behavior can cause the other person to develop psychological trauma, including anxiety, depression, and post-traumatic stress disorder. It is deliberately done with the purpose of weakening or frightening a person mentally and emotionally or with the purpose of manipulation, i.e. to distort, confuse, or influence a person's thoughts and actions.

Verbal abuse is included within this category of offenses since the perpetrator often makes use of non-physical tactics to make the victim feel diminished and humiliated. Psychological abuse is known to increase the trauma of physical and sexual abuse, and it can even independently cause long-term damage to a person's mental health. Statistics show that 48.4% of all women and 48.8% of all men have experienced at least one instance of psychologically aggressive behavior by their intimate partner.[36] Psychological abuse can include:

- Humiliation

- Enforced social isolation, i.e. preventing someone from seeing friends and accessing services and educational and social opportunities

---

[36] National Coalition Against Domestic Violence. (n.d.). If you need help: Call The National Domestic Violence Hotline 1–800–799–SAFE (7233) Or, online go to DomesticShelters.org Suggested citation: NCADV. (2015). Facts about domestic violence and psychological abuse. Retrieved from www.ncadv.org Facts about Domestic Violence and Psychological Abuse. NCADV. Retrieved September 21, 2021, from https://assets.speakcdn.com/assets/2497/domestic_violence_and_psychological_ab use_ncadv.pdf

- Manipulation, i.e. controlling what the victim can or cannot do

- Deliberately doing something to make the victim feel small, weak, and embarrassed

- Failure to respect the victim's privacy

- Undermining the victim's sense of self-worth

- Intentionally leaving someone unattended, especially when you know they need assistance

- Preventing someone from freely practicing and fulfilling their religious and cultural needs

- Undermining the victim's freedom of expression, choice, and opinion

- Intimidation and bullying

- Coercive behavior, i.e. use of threats and emotional manipulation to get what you want

- Swearing and verbal abuse

- Demeaning a person in public or private

- Denying the person access to money or other basic resources

- Stalking and withholding information from the victim

Indicators of psychological or emotional abuse include:

• Signs of distress, i.e. anger, frustration, tearfulness, easy stimulation

• Unnecessary seeking of attention and validation

- Low self-esteem

- Uncooperative and aggressive behavior

- Sleep disturbances

- Withdrawal from social activities

- Changes in the psychological state of the person

- Change in appetite; sudden gain or loss of weight

- Signs of constant anxiety or depression

Financial or Material Abuse

Financial or material abuse involves the illegal or unauthorized use of a person's money, property, pension book, or other valuables. It also involves controlling a person's ability to acquire, use, and maintain their financial resources.

A study done by the Centers for Financial Security found that almost 99% of domestic violence cases also involved some form of financial abuse.[37] It has also been recorded that women who earn 65% or more of their household income are more likely to be psychologically abused than women who earn less than 65%. Financial abuse can include:

- Theft of money or valuable possessions

- Undue pressure, threat, or influence put on a person in connection with loan, property, inheritance, or financial transactions

---

[37] Gordon, S. G. (2020, May 6). How to Identify Financial Abuse in a Relationship. Very Well Minded. https://www.verywellmind.com/financial-abuse-4155224

- Misuse or stealing of personal allowance in a care home

- Denying assistance to access benefits in the workplace

- Preventing the victim from accessing their money, benefits, or assets

- False representation done by the unauthorized use of another person's bank account, cards, or documents

- Misuse of benefits or direct payments in a family home

- Trying to control your use or access of the money that you have earned or saved

- Using another person's credit card without permission

- Using your assets for their personal benefits without permission

- Borrowing money or making charges without any repayment

- Forcing a person to turn over their paycheck, credit card(s), or passwords

- Ruining someone's credit history by reaching the limit and then not paying bills

- Trying to gain control of your finances by offering help with your budget and financial decisions

- Confiscating your paychecks or any other monetary support

- Unauthorized access to bank statements and other financial records

- Criticizing your financial decisions and reducing your freedom to plan and budget

- Taking funds and putting them in a private account

- Pressuring you to quit your job, sometimes using children as an excuse

- Refusing to work and contribute to the family income

- Forcing victims to sign financial documents without giving any explanations

Financial abuse in relationships is often done to gain control and keep the victim trapped in an abusive relationship. Financial insecurity is known to be one of the biggest reasons why women usually return to abusive partners. Indications of material abuse include:

- Missing personal possessions

- The person who is supposed to be managing your financial affairs is evasive or uncooperative

- Lasting power of attorney (LPA) being obtained after the person has been deemed mentally unfit to manage their finances

- Family or other close friends/ peers showing unusual interest in the financial assets of a person

- A lack of clear financial records held by a care home or service

- The disparity between the person's living conditions and their financial resources

- Recent changes in title to property or deeds

- Failure to provide receipts for financial transactions carried out on behalf of another person

- Victim having to give an account of every minute spending

- The abuser may be subtle and highly manipulative or maybe overtly demanding and threatening

Neglect and Acts of Omission

Neglect and acts of omission include the failure of any person who has been given the responsibility for the charge, care, and custody of another person, whether it be a child or an adult at risk, to provide the optimum type of care that any reasonable person would be required to give. Neglect can be both intentional and unintentional, but it is abusive.

According to the U.S. Department of Health and Human Services, neglect has been accounted for more than three-quarters of the confirmed cases of child maltreatment in the United States, which is far more than physical or sexual abuse.[38] Types of neglect can include physical neglect, medical neglect, inadequate supervision, emotional neglect, and educational neglect. Neglect and acts of omission can include:

- Failure to provide or allow access to proper food, clothing, shelter, heating, personal and medical care

- Refusing visitors

---

[38] Child Welfare Information Gateway. (n.d.). Acts of Omission: An Overview of Child Neglect. Retrieved September 21, 2021, from https://www.childwelfare.gov/pubs/focus/acts/

- Not taking into account the person's cultural, religious, or ethnic needs

- Not taking into account the person's educational, social, and recreational needs

- Ignoring or isolating the person

- Not being sensitive toward the person's likes and dislikes while caring for them

- Preventing the person from making their decisions when they are capable of making rightful decisions for themselves

- Failure to administer medications as prescribed

- Failure to ensure privacy and maintenance of the other person's dignity

- Preventing access to glasses, dentures, hearing aids, or other stuff that they need that are necessary for their day–to–day life

- Ignoring medical, emotional, or physical care needs

- Any act or failure to act on the part of the caretaker which results in the death, serious physical or emotional harm, sexual abuse, or exploitation of the victim

Indicators for neglect and acts of omission can include:

- Malnutrition and unexplained weight loss

- Poor living conditions; dirty or unhygienic environment

- Untreated injuries and frequent medical problems

- Pressure sores and ulcers

- Inadequate heating and lighting

- Failure to socially engage with the person being cared for

- Accumulation of untaken prescription of medication

- The ill-fitting, unclean, or poor condition of clothing

- Failure to provide appropriate privacy

- Signs of distress, frustration, and anger

- Change in a psychological state of a person

- Inconsistent contact with health and social care agencies[39]

What Is Domestic Violence?

Domestic violence is a pattern of abusive behavior where the victim being violated is within the domestic circle of the perpetrator. This can include partners, ex-partners, parents, children, grandparents, other relatives, and even family friends. There are many categories of domestic violence, including intimate partner abuse, child abuse, senior abuse, and honor-based violence.

The latter can include things such as honor killings, female genital mutilations (also called 'female circumcision), and forced marriages. At first, domestic violence was referred to as wife abuse. However, this label was soon abandoned to adopt a broader term that was inclusive of all the victims within the

---

[39] Types and indicators of abuse. (2015, January). Social Care Institute for Excellence. https://www.scie.org.uk/safeguarding/adults/introduction/types-and-indicators-of-abuse

domestic sphere. [40] Domestic violence encompasses all the types of abuse that we discussed above, as long as they occur within the domestic sphere. The victim can suffer from physical, emotional, sexual, and financial abuse, along with negligence at the hands of their intimate partner, caregiver, family member, or sibling. Four in 10 women and four in 10 men have experienced coercive control by their intimate partners in their lifetime.

17.9% of women have experienced a situation where their intimate partners tried to keep them from seeing their family and friends. Thus, domestic and family violence is a widespread problem in the United States, impacting an estimated 10 million people each year. One in every four women and one in every nine males are victims of domestic abuse.

Why Do People Struggle to Confront Their Abusers?

Despite the fact that domestic abuse is so prevalent, not many people can find it in themselves to leave those abusive situations. This can be due to many reasons, including fear, financial insecurity, emotional and psychological entrapment, or political control. People often don't even realize they are living in abusive situations or try to justify their abuse by believing that the abuse was well deserved. This 'deserving and undeserving victim' dilemma is what prevents many people from doing something about their abuse.

---

[40] United Nations Organization. (n.d.). What Is Domestic Abuse? United Nations. Retrieved September 21, 2021, from https://www.un.org/en/coronavirus/what-is-domestic-abuse

Several of these people believe that it is okay to be slapped, kicked, or punched, even to the point of severe damage, as long as there is some reason for them to be deserving of this damage. The "undeserving victim" thus doesn't view abuse as abuse, but rather as punishment. It is only when these people realize that they are being wronged, do they find the courage to stand up for themselves or at least feel anger that shifts their attitude toward the situation and makes them want to escape.

In today's time, people with a public profile or a public relationship might also feel threatened by their high status and stay in abusive relationships for longer periods. In such relationships, the victim might avoid speaking up in fear of either ruining their partner's career or not being believed. Even though the idea of domestic abuse has now become increasingly frowned upon by the general public, there is still a lot of social stigmas attached to it. This stigma is mostly tied to sexist views and victim shaming.

A study published in the Journal of Personality and Social Psychology found that bystanders viewed assault over an intimate partner as less severe than assault over a stranger, even if the damage was of the same degree.[41] This only demonstrates the hyper-normalization of domestic violence. Many times, people are caught in the midst of isolating and confidence-crushing abuse which completely makes them doubt their self-worth. They are made to think that no one will believe them if they open up about their abuse or that they will

---

[41] R.L., & M.K. (n.d.). Bystander response to an assault: When a man attacks a woman. APA PsycNet. Retrieved September 29, 2021, from
https://psycnet.apa.org/record/1977-10327-001

be dismissed or called names. They are told that they won't have anywhere to go and are completely intimidated and belittled into staying. What makes it worse is when they are met with indifference from others and are given insults that add to their injuries. Sometimes abuse is hidden due to fear of social stigma or fear of a threat to the family name or image. Sometimes, the victims are psychologically manipulated.

This especially happens in the case of intimate partner violence when the partner abuses the victim and then tries to apologize and make it up to them by being kind, sensitive, and considerate. This creates a hot and cold situation where the victim feels overwhelmed and can't get themselves to leave the person for their momentary flaws and instead tries to see the "good" they have in them and stays. These people often hold onto the unreasonable hope that their partner might change their ways every time they apologize. But the truth of the matter is, people of abuse rarely change their ways. It is better to walk away in this case and let them hold onto the hope that you may return when they get better.

In reality, however, it isn't that easy to be able to leave behind a toxic person. There is often the constant fear that the person will find them, and the abuse and stalking will continue, if not escalate. According to a paper published in the second edition of the *Case Studies in Family Violence*, it was found that the risk of homicide increases for a certain period of time after a woman decides to leave her abusive intimate partner.[42]

---

[42] Saunders, D. S., & Browne, A. B. (2000). Intimate Partner Homicide (No. 18). Harvard School of Public Health, Boston.

Not surprisingly, this renders people helpless and too afraid to do anything. Domestic abuse is a serious threat, especially to women, yet it is so easily overlooked and dismissed. Domestic abuse victims need to be provided with some sort of security or protection, and this is why security agencies need to up their game and start looking for ways to help people escape these kinds of situations.

Sometimes, abuse can only be countered with the use of force, so security officers must specially be trained in order to be able to deal with such incidents. It is important that the officer understands the use of force continuum regarding how, when, and what type of force may be used against a threat.

---

https://deepblue.lib.umich.edu/bitstream/handle/2027.42/116793/Saunders%20%26%20Browne%202000%20Intimate%20Partner%20Homicide%20Chapt%2018%20in%20Case%20Studies%20in%20Family%20Violence%20-%20Springer%20.pdf?sequence=1&isAllowed=y

Chapter 6: Unsafe Neighborhoods

Crime has existed everywhere for as long as the dawn of civilization. It has created chaos and disorder in communities for centuries and continues to do so even today. One thing that has intrigued criminologists for a very long time is finding the root cause of this curse.

One can easily point out the many various reasons why crime can be prevalent in a place. It could be due to generational poverty, lack of education, and a rupture in the community structure. These reasons were deduced from statistics showing a higher crime rate in poor inner-city neighborhoods than the more affluent ones.

A theory was devised using these statistics, which was called the broken window theory. Two social scientists named James Q. Wilson and George L. Kelling introduced this theory in an article titled "Broken Windows" in the March 1982 issue of *The Atlantic Monthly*. They wrote:

"At the community level, disorder and crime are usually inextricably linked, in a kind of developmental sequence. Social psychologists and police officers tend to agree that if a window in a building is broken and is left unrepaired, all the rest of the windows will soon be broken. This is as true in nice neighborhoods as in rundown ones. Window-breaking does not necessarily occur on a large scale because some areas are inhabited by determined window-breakers whereas others are populated by window-lovers; rather, one unrepaired broken window is a signal that no one cares, and so breaking more windows costs nothing. (It has always been

fun.)."[43] *The theory states that any visible indicators of disorder, such as vandalism, loitering, public drinking, jaywalking, and fare evasion, create an urban environment that encourages anti-social and criminal behavior by way of letting people know that there will be no consequences of their deviance.*

It hints toward the absence of law and order and thus, people automatically assume that their chances of being held accountable for doing something bad are very low. That is to say, the presence of one broken window can lead to the rest being broken in no time.

The way that this theory works depends upon three factors:

- Social norms and conformity

- The presence or lack of routine monitoring

- Social signaling and signal crime

Suppose a person is in an anonymous urban environment where there are no people monitoring the social situation, and the norms are not clearly known. In that case, the person looks for signals within the environment to see which norms are followed here and which aren't.

The first thing the said person could judge their environment is by looking at the area's general appearance. Under the broken window theory, a clean and well-maintained environment allows the person to appreciate that no criminal behavior is tolerated here. On the other hand, if something's out of order, it

---

[43] Kelling, G. K., & Wilson, J. W. (1982, March 1). Broken Windows; The police and neighborhood safety. The Atlantic. https://www.theatlantic.com/magazine/archive/1982/03/broken-windows/304465/

sends a message that this sort of behavior is tolerated and thus will hold no consequences. This theory was used to develop policing tactics, such as foot patrol and higher community engagement, that were put to practice on many different occasions, and they supposedly led to a decrease in overall crime reports and an increase in public safety.

Supporters of this theory claim that it enabled the criminal justice system to develop less expensive and quick police crime-control strategies, which have been tested in previous case studies like the 2005 study in Lowell, Massachusetts. In this study, researchers from Harvard University and Suffolk University worked with local police officers and identified 34 crime hotspots in Lowell, Massachusetts.

In half of these areas, authorities were told to make small and seemingly indistinct changes such as cleaning up trash from the streets, fixing the streetlights, expanding mental health services, aiding the homeless, making more misdemeanor arrests discourage loiterers, and enforcing building codes. While in the other half, there was no change in routine police activities.

It was found that in areas where the changes were made, there was a 20% reduction in phone calls to the police. This proved that people felt safer being in an environment that was more organized, which means cleaning up the environment can be very effective in reducing public fear. But the results were somewhat insignificant as they were only seen because the police officers were having greater interactions with the community, so all their complaints were already being heard.

It was not so much a reduction in crime as it was an improvement on behalf of the availability of the officers. Although many people would argue that the broken window theory is not worth all the praise, it gets and has only become a vehicle for discrimination today.

With these crime-controlling methods being predominated by informal social control, police are carrying out more arrests based on false assumptions of crime and misdemeanor. The stop and frisk, which is known to be a brief and non-intrusive inspection of a suspect, has now become increasingly controversial as it has proven to be unsuccessful.

A report from 2008 showed that the police made almost 250,000 stops in New York, but only one-fifteenth of one percent of those stops resulted in finding a gun. Despite this, many police agencies still operate with the broken window tactics, even when they have been proven not to be as effective as they were thought to be.[44]

This is all for public crime and overt signs of a disorder. Domestic violence, however, does not fit into this perspective at all. It is hidden behind closed doors and often goes unreported. Sometimes, matters of domestic violence are even dismissed and not considered as big enough offenses to require legal intervention. Therefore, the broken window theory does not account for all types of crimes and thus, is not good if considered alone while drawing policies for the criminal justice system.

---

[44] Ruhl, C. R. (2021, July 26). The Broken Windows Theory. Simply Psychology. https://www.simplypsychology.org/broken-windows-theory.html

Of course, pre-Covid domestic violence was predominantly found in low-income or poorer neighborhoods. Only about 1% of the city used to be targeted with this issue, and a lot of it was tied to neighborhoods that already fit into the broken window description. The rest of the community was too busy living their lives and was not previously bothered by problems like lack of healthcare and poverty.

On the other hand, during this quarantine period, every person was tested with such problems, which led to a surge in domestic abuse reports. So it was this pandemic that helped us recognize our society's inherently detrimental ways and has also brought to light the ineffectiveness of our prior policing methods. Since everybody is locked up at home, not many crimes are taking place outside, so you cannot see any broken windows that need fixing.

But the truth is, violent crimes are still happening. They just continue to stay hidden behind those perfectly fixed windows that security agencies so easily seem to ignore. For example, I did my 21st domestic violence detail recently, and the area did not have a bunch of broken windows or any other apparent sign of disorder. So, this is something that social workers, police officers, and even policymakers need to focus on more.

With Covid, people weren't able to get out and socialize, and they were stuck at home with their families, so, unsurprisingly, the domestic violence rate went up, but with the effects of the pandemic still resonating everywhere, domestic violence has persisted.

One of my client's, a woman who lives in Palm Beach, was trying to get out of her home and get away from a guy who had been physically and verbally abusing her, but it was hard for her to legally get any help because nobody was able to see that crime taking place, so it was essentially just her word against his. It was a very abusive environment, so much so that the woman's daughter, who came in from Maryland to live with her mother, now has PTSD from the trauma this man has induced upon them.

Law enforcement was not able to do anything. She could not even get a court order to evict him, which she tried doing since it was her home. Thus, we can stand by the claim that domestic violence is not restricted to seemingly unsafe neighborhoods. It's a plague that spreads all over, without any regard to the financial or educational background of a household.

For so many years, law enforcement focused on targeting areas that are "hot spots of criminal activity" for crimes such as gun violence, robberies, homicides, etc. However, we can no longer recognize crimes by judging the environment or setting of an area, and we should no longer be targeting marginalized communities for our suspicions. This pandemic has made it glaringly obvious that crime is not limited to the non-domestic circle and it is most certainly not restricted within unsafe neighborhoods.

Chapter 7: A Safe Place

"If social disorganization is the problem and if traditional agents of social control no longer are performing adequately, we need to find alternative ways to strengthen informal social control and restore a 'sense of neighborhood.'" **–Rosenbaum, 1988**

Criminologists and policymakers very often seek to develop tools for security professionals to help them deal with the various types of threats there are to the security of citizens. But as we discussed in the previous chapters, when it comes to assault and violence that takes place behind closed doors, it's hard to confront or even detect these cases. With the broken window theory failing to provide security agencies with any lucrative or viable policing options, the best course of action would be to employ an improved version of the Neighborhood Watch Program on a larger scale all over the U.S.

The Neighborhood Watch Program is one of the oldest and the most effective means available for keeping crime out of neighborhoods. It is also commonly known as "crime watch", "block watch", "business watch", or "homeowner's association". The Neighborhood Watch Program was created by the National Sheriffs' Association (NSA) in 1972 after the surge in crime in the late 1960s.[45] It was a crime prevention initiative created with the purpose of making neighborhoods safer. It relies on a group of people living in the same area who want to

---

[45] National Neighborhood Watch: A Division of the National Sheriffs' Association. (n.d.). What Is Neighborhood Watch? National Neighborhood Watch. Retrieved October 19, 2021, from https://www.nnw.org/what-neighborhood-watch

make their neighborhood safer and have some kind of experience in this domain, working in conjunction with the local law enforcement officers to make sure that everything is in place within the neighborhood. Neighborhood watch groups have assigned leaders, and they carry out regular meetings to plan out their specific goals and how they will accomplish them. Each person in the group has a set of responsibilities such as hosting meetings, enrolling new members, fund-raising, secretarial duties, crime prevention material distribution, etc. It is homeland security at the most local residential level.

It is true that a nation is built on the strength of its citizens. Like Anna Sewell said, *"It is good people who make good places."*

Therefore, allowing the people to get involved in their security measures will ensure that those measures take effect. The watch groups do not advocate for its members to take any action when they see criminal activity as that might put the members at risk. The community members still act as extra eyes and ears and help report all kinds of suspicious businesses that might be taking place in their neighborhood. This is because every person can contribute to a watch program.

The plus side of this is that the residents of a community are more aware of what's going on inside their neighborhood. Such things as domestic and gun violence are more likely to come upfront earlier and be dealt with. The power of different members of the community working together to prevent crime in their area is almost as effective, if not more, as deploying contracted guards 24/7.

A negative side is most neighborhoods cannot afford to hire contract guards or police officers on 24/7 watch. These neighborhoods do not have the funds, and law enforcement agencies do not have the manpower to allocate a crime prevention officer for this program.

Now, the difference between using broken window tactics and using a neighborhood watch group is that with the former, there was little to no involvement of the community in the establishment of social control. It was all done by the police, who tried to get rid of things that might "potentially" create disorder. This meant that the police officer's bias could easily come into play here, and the strict check and balance and regulation systems meant that more people were getting arrested.

The police officers can easily abuse their authority in such a condition, and it could be extremely detrimental to the community members, especially if the citizens and police officers aren't on the same page.

How Exactly Does the Neighborhood Watch Program Work?

The Neighborhood Watch Program places great emphasis on educating and teaching citizens and community members how to help themselves by identifying and reporting suspicious activity in their neighborhoods. It focuses on observation and awareness to prevent crime and employs strategies such as active patrols, guided training sessions, and instructive meetings. Most of the time, the crime prevention group is organized around a block or a neighborhood and starts with the assistance of a law enforcement agency.

One major issue is, as stated earlier, the limited number of police officers to effectively run or oversee crime prevention programs in neighborhoods. Additionally, neighborhood volunteers do not have the skills necessary to develop and run a neighborhood crime prevention program.

A viable option would be to hire a security agency to be the neighborhood watch leader and develop and run your neighborhood watch program. Most of these agencies employ former law enforcement and military personnel with crime prevention skills and experience. I strongly advise all communities to seek out security agencies to establish and run their programs. If the neighborhood requires funds to pay for this program, I suggest two possible methods:

1. **Refunding the police:** No one wants to defund the police, but refunding police agencies is an option. Reallocating funds through this channel (and others) to neighborhoods plagued with violence can help pay for a contracted professional security agency.

2. **Barter fixed cost:** Bartering service for a cost is another technique to attract a security agency. Normally, that major fixed cost is an office with a conference room. The security agency would conduct all security guard and neighborhood watch training and presentations from this location.

While the activities conducted by these neighborhood watch groups are diverse and vary excessively across the country, most of them prevent or reduce crime following these two major approaches; *opportunity reduction* and *social problems.*

Opportunity Reduction

This approach focuses on crime reduction by observing informal social control in order to restore a 'sense of neighborhood'. The Watch members place stickers over their windows and post Neighborhood Watch signs on the streets. This way, the criminals are warned that they are in an active Neighborhood Watch community. This helps to deter anyone who thinks of committing a crime in the neighborhood since they know they are being watched and might get caught.

Even in cases of domestic violence, the abusers know that the members of the community will try to intervene by checking in or they will make a call to the authorities and report their misdemeanor.

Again, apathy is fuel for criminals, whether they're the ones inside your home or the ones who are trying to break in. If they know that someone's going to bust them, it makes them more alert and less likely to commit the crime. The watch groups also mobilize to patrol neighborhoods and do frequent business assessments and home security surveys. Thus, there are reduced opportunities for unwarranted behavior and criminal activity.

Social Problems

This approach focuses on addressing certain issues in the neighborhood that might be linked with higher levels of crime.

These social problems are addressed by conducting youth-targeted programs such as athletic activities, tutoring, drug programs, conducting neighborhood cleanups, or working with faith-based organizations to assist the panhandlers, homeless, and the mentally ill.

How to Start a Neighborhood Watch Group?

This program is a proactive method of fighting crime, and it hands the primary responsibility of conducting social control to the community members. If you live in the United States and wish to start a watch group in your neighborhood, I suggest that your community leaders contact a security agency for assistance. Because violence is so prevalent in our society, it will require detailed planning and execution of security agencies and volunteers for this program to succeed.

In the end, a successful program can help keep your community protected at times of crisis or emergency and can keep you safe from crime. It will require maximum neighborhood participation so everyone will know the concerns of the community and about the program's crime and safety benefits. A communication plan can accomplish this.

Develop an Effective Communication Plan

A communication plan can be an effective way to help target your message to the neighborhood. It can "influence the efficiency and simplicity of your communication methods". Not only can this method raise awareness, but it can also be an excellent way to get more volunteers. I suggest starting the communication plan while you are developing the goals, objectives, and activities for the neighborhood.

There are many ways to communicate the goals and objectives to the neighborhood community, including:

- Talking face to face to your neighbors

- Providing neighborhood news stories to the community on print, broadcast, and social media platforms

- Providing press releases and press conferences to special events, activities, open houses, and neighborhood watch meetings

- Creating and using posters, flyers, banners, and brochures when needed

- Connecting with law enforcement, health and community service providers, security companies, community groups, and other organizations to build relationships

It helps to plan the goals and expectations from your communication plan and modify them if they aren't being met.

The first neighborhood watch meeting should include all criminal activities in the last 10 years and start developing a crime prevention strategy. This strategy will guide the communication plan of action and provide a means to assess and evaluate its effectiveness.

There are several ways in which you can educate and motivate the neighborhood in crime prevention. These methods are online as well as in person. After all the goals, objectives, and communication plans of action have been determined, security agencies, leaders, law enforcement, and volunteers should schedule frequent meetings and continue training the community on policing and crime prevention. The National Sheriffs' Association has an excellent online self-paced training program "designed to build the individual skills of the law enforcers, public service officer, or Neighborhood Watch leader". This program emphasizes exploring neighborhood cleanup days and patrols, business vulnerability studies, regular home surveys, and seminars on terrorism prevention and national disaster safety. I suggest adding the following items to update the program.

SALUTE Reports

The SALUTE report is an excellent template used by the military to quickly capture important information about the enemy activity. The SALUTE acronym stands for situation, activity, location, uniform, time, and equipment present. This reporting platform can be modified to report and record suspicious activity in the area. However, when that information is supported with photos and videos, it becomes a tangible asset for law enforcement to track and arrest criminals.

Statistical Crime Reports

This report provides quarterly crime statistics and addresses and modifies the crime prevention techniques being used to reduce the crime. This report can serve as one of the key performance indicators (KPI) of the strategic plan for the neighborhood watch community. The FBI Uniform Crime Reporting (UCR) has been compiling crime stats for over 90 years. Additionally, the FBI's Crime Data Explorer (CDE) will enable the neighborhood watch groups to establish charts and graphs to better explain criminal activity in the area.

Gun and Home Safety Classes

Did you know that 15 of the last 168 mass shootings in America could have been prevented if parents would have secured their firearms? Therefore, providing free gun and home safety classes, which include safe handling and storage of firearms and ammo, would be essential to help mitigate gun and neighborhood violence.

Situational Awareness Training

Situational Awareness is a mindset of "being aware of what is happening around you in terms of where you are, where you are supposed to be, and whether anyone or anything around you is a threat to your health and safety (www.hse.gov.ik)". It is a good way to detect, recognize, identify (SALUTE reports), and understand suspicious neighborhood activity. The community will learn how to use their cell phones to capture and report potential criminal activity in the neighborhood.

Neighborhood Watch Mobile Applications

A neighborhood mobile app can be the perfect platform to report potential criminal activity. It is imperative for neighborhood watch leaders to develop or use an existing App and make it available for the residence of that neighborhood. It should operate similar to next door, except this app should enable the user to quickly record only questionable and criminal types of activities in an easy format.

Crime Prevention Newsletters

This provides an online and hard copy of the crime prevention newsletter with monthly, quarterly, and annual information about criminal activity, crime prevention policies and programs, and other security issues.

I used this effective communication technique while working as the provost marshal in the military. When I opened my first security company in Toledo, Ohio in 2005, I remember creating and distributing hundreds of newsletters to explain the crime prevention plan and provide tips on combatting criminal activities in the community.

Additionally, I used this pre-online method to coordinate monthly neighborhood watch meetings with the community, their leaders, and law enforcement to address the crimes and concerns of the neighborhood. Within the first six months, there was a 60% drop in overall crime. The after-action report revealed that adding new neighborhood watch signs, keeping the neighborhood informed about local crime, and providing crime prevention tips were significant in reducing crime in that community.

Train Guards and Volunteers

Training the agency's security guards, executive protection team, and volunteer patrols in the neighborhood is another way to help reduce crime. The knowledge and presence of security and volunteers working and training together to reduce neighborhood crime will rally the community. Agencies can use this training opportunity to conduct first aid, self-defense, physical training, situational awareness, crime prevention, reporting procedures, etc.

Surveillance

Surveillance is an excellent way to monitor and record neighborhood activity. Post cameras and CCTV where needed and allow the neighborhood access to view current and past recordings. Also, record cars entering the neighborhood and coordinate safety measures for homeowners, especially if they are leaving town.

Cybercrimes

Internet and shopping fraud, stalking, identity theft, child soliciting, hacking, etc. are global threats designed to steal primarily personal assets, money, and even lives. Young adults (under 25), old adults (over 75), women, and minorities are most likely to be victims of cybercrime. It is very important to educate the communities about cybercrime and provide the necessary countermeasures.

Chapter 8: Resources in Hand

Like any other profession, security professionals need resources too. These platforms and resources are necessary for various reasons, but the most important resource is your brain. It has the ability to understand and follow complex instructions. It is what makes a security professional vigilant and effective.

It is also important for a security officer to have a basic knowledge of computers and know how to use the internet. In this modern world, technology is overtaking every profession in the world. There was a time when all investigations were done in person or by phone. Nowadays, fieldwork for security professionals has changed due to the availability of the internet. So, it is necessary for security professionals to understand how to use this resource to their advantage.

Internet/Website

The internet (specifically Google) is the most important resource for many reasons. It can provide unlimited information on various topics and can be used for off-site training. Additionally, Google maps provide even the most minute details about different locations. There is hardly any person in the world who doesn't use the internet for social media. Their online presence can give you a lot of insights into their lives.

Internet is so vast that even CCTV camera videos can be viewed and shared over the network and accessed when needed. Your website would be a great asset in providing you with the market for people to hire you. You can advertise your website through Google to drive enough traffic toward your website. The possibilities are endless.

ASIS International

American Society for Industrial Security (ASIS) is a global community for professional security practitioners who have the same mission of protecting people, property, and information. This international organization provides research material and helps establish standards and guidelines for the security profession. It also uses the internet to connect people and businesses in the security industry worldwide.

Health and Safety

Health and safety are crucial at workplaces. The OHS (Occupational Health and Safety) is a multidisciplinary field that studies the trends in illnesses and injuries in the worker population. It also imposes implementation strategies and regulations to prevent them.

Cybersecurity Drive

Police and security provide the necessary physical security to their customers or people in the neighborhood, but citizens also have personal information which can be breached and accessed by hackers. Therefore, security professionals should have basic knowledge of cybersecurity to counter the cyberthreats their clients could face. A lot of confidential information resides in their PCs. Cybersecurity is a resource that could help them secure critical information from digital attacks.

Global Security

Global security, also known as international security, refers to the measures taken by states and international organizations, like that of NATO, UN, EU, and others, to ensure mutual survival and safety. This organization provides threat and risk analyses that allow policymakers to identify political, military, and economic trends around the world. They also identify potential regional conflicts and concerns which can help with strategic planning.

YouTube

YouTube is the most beneficial resource for officers to train themselves. Thousands of videos are available on this site. You can use this material to support your agency's training plan.

Smartphone

Your smartphone can be used to access the internet and as a backup to the handheld radio. It can be used to capture data for electronic reporting for the Daily Activity Reports (DAR) and Incident Reports (IR).

On-the-Job Training (OJT)

Another great resource is to utilize the experience of other security officers to provide on-the-job training of new hires on-site. This saves time and money for formal training and helps to determine if the new hire is capable of successfully accomplishing the mission.

The following skills are taught and evaluated during the OJT program:

1. Computer skills
2. Lifting and walking
3. Objectivity
4. Judgment abilities
5. Multitasking
6. Written and oral communication
7. Security operations and procedures
8. Surveillance skills
9. Professionalism
10. Safety protocols and management
11. Patrolling
12. Reporting and documenting skills

Threat, Risk, and Vulnerability Assessments

The TRVA aims to protect people's assets and minimize the exposure to crime and terrorism in their neighborhoods. It also helps to better understand the behavior pattern of the abuser in order to determine what security and business risks they present.

These assessments involve a comprehensive and critical problem-solving evaluation of a client's entire security framework. This includes a detailed study of the threat and the risk, charting vulnerabilities and providing solutions to the vulnerabilities, among many other things. The threat, risk, and vulnerability assessments are the most significant parts of a short- and long-term planning process in Troop Leading Procedures and Strategic Planning.

Security Response Plan for Abusive and Violent Situations

It is imperative that leaders develop a plan before responding to these emergencies. A well-designed plan works as a critical tool used to help define the risk while providing direction, goals, and courses of action for the team. I use the Troop Leading Procedures (TLP) format for short-term planning and a more comprehensive long-term plan for Strategic Planning.

Troop Leading Procedures

Many domestic disturbances become violent by the time we are contacted. For those emergencies that need our immediate attention, I use the TLP format after receiving the mission. The Troop Leading Procedures (TLP) is a proven small unit military planning process designed to quickly analyze, prepare, and execute security operations. This dynamic problem-solving process can be modified when necessary to meet the requirements of the mission. The eight-step TLP process is:

Step 1: Receive the Mission

The mission begins by receiving an email, phone call, or a face-to-face meeting, addressing the need for protection services. The client will provide a lot of valuable information about the situation and the threat for you to make a quick tentative plan. I highly suggest that you record the conversation. Always try to gather all the information available for sound decision-making and planning. The more information you obtain on the subject(s) and everyone else connected to the situation, the better to completely understand the requirements to complete the mission successfully (estimate of the situation).

You can use the internet as the initial research tool to gather more information. Here are just a few items I use Google for when gathering information on the subject to use in the METT-TC planning guide:

- Name check

- Background check

- License plates check

- Social media check

- Address check

- Neighborhood check

I use an improvised version of the METT-TC as a planning guide to initially analyze the mission. It enables me to capture important information of the mission and research, analyze, and estimate the desired courses of action. METT-TC stands for mission, enemy, terrain, troops, time, and civilians.

- **Mission:** The who, what, when, where, why, and how provide a clear understanding of the situation and the goals necessary to successfully complete them. It becomes the mission statement for the Operations Order.

- **Enemy:** Conduct detailed research on the abuser to better understand what level of risk and threat they pose for the mission. What is their profession? Have they been arrested in the past? Do they own firearms? Is this an isolated incident or a pattern? How many people are involved? What are their capabilities? Ensure that you get the correct names and addresses of everyone involved and the DOB of the abuser. Have the client spell names if you have any questions. That information will allow you to conduct background checks when necessary to determine how serious of a threat they are to your team and the client.

- **Terrain:** A vulnerability assessment of the home, yard, and neighborhood may be necessary to determine if the abuser's avenue to approach to potentially stalk and ambush the victim. I use Google Earth, neighborhood layouts, and housing information to conduct a very basic recon for vulnerability analysis. Later on, a more comprehensive vulnerability analysis may be done on-site. Additionally, you can identify key terrain and obstacles present to restrict or impede movement.

- **Troops**: This section determines the number and the right-skilled protection officer needed for the mission.

- **Time:** This phase identifies the necessary time needed for planning, training (if required), traveling, eating, sleeping, etc.

- **Civilians:** What type of neighborhood does the client reside in? Do they have a neighborhood watch program or HOA? Is the client (or abuser) friends with their neighbors? Are they an asset or threat? This information is valuable on how to interact with the civilians in the area.

Step 2: Issue a Warning Order

The WO is a brief but complete advanced notice to your team of an upcoming mission. It is normally done after the initial assessment. The format is the same as the five-paragraph operation order used to complete the plan, except it may need to be updated and refined. It is very important to provide the WO to your team as soon as possible to allow for maximum preparation. The components of the five-paragraph operations order are Situation, Mission, Execution, Command and Signal, and Service and Support.

Step 3: Make a Tentative Plan

Make a tentative plan. Understanding the situation and the mission will enable you to determine the basic concept of the operation. It is important to complete the initial plan as quickly as possible. You may see the situation constantly changing, so be prepared to update and refine the WO. This could be completed with a FRAGO or an OPORD. The five steps to making a tentative plan are[46]:

1. Detailed mission analysis

2. Situation analysis and course of action development

3. Analysis of each course of action

4. Comparison of each course of action

5. Decision

Step 4: Initiate Movement

This addresses any movement of the team to prepare and execute the mission. I always lead the movement to better access the situation to complete the plan.

Step 5: Conduct Reconnaissance

When time allows, I personally view the location before executing the mission. The reconnaissance provides valuable intelligence about the situation. If that cannot be done, then the reconnaissance can be done when the team arrives. Nothing substitutes for observing where the team is to operate.

Step 6: Complete the Plan

Once the reconnaissance and the estimation of the situation are completed, you can complete the plan. That plan should focus on protecting the client while helping to establish

---

[46] Anon. n.d. "MVOrganizing – Knowledge Bank: Quick Advice for Everyone." Retrieved January 18, 2022 (https://www.mvorganizing.org/)

corrective methods. It should include the use of force plan-based TRVA.

Step 7: Issue the Order

The operations order is normally the final order issued for the mission. I prefer issuing the order face to face so I can immediately answer questions and concerns from the team and get feedback from them. I also provide a separate verbal presentation to the client for their support and approval.

Step 8: Supervise, Inspect, and Refine

The operations order is a fluid document, so expect to continuously update the order as you collect and analyze more information about the situation.

Format for the WO and OPORD

The Warning and Operations Orders are the plans presented to the team to execute the mission. As previously stated, they follow the same format except for the issue of the WO being time-sensitive. The following is an example of how the five-paragraph WO/OPORD can be used in security:

1. **Situation**: The situation paragraph contains the information on the overall status of friendly and enemy personnel involved. The information is vital to understanding the current situation.

   a. *Enemy Forces*: Information about the weather, lighting, and the abuser is provided in this section. It should be the culmination of intelligence provided by the victim and researched online. The abuser's situation can be issued by using the SALUTE reporting acronym. (See chapter, *Neighborhood Watch Program*).

   i. Situation (enemy, weather, and terrain).

  ii. Capabilities – (firearms, drug-induced, etc.)

 iii. The probable course of action – (fight, flee, no show, etc.)

  b. *Friendly Forces*: This information is geared toward anyone or any agency that provides assistance and support for the victim.

   i. The mission of other supporting units – police, lawyers, courts

  ii. The mission of adjacent units – N/A

 iii. Mission and location of supporting elements

  c. *Attachments and Detachments*

  2. **Mission**: The mission statement is a clear and concise statement usually containing one sentence which answers the who (unit), what (task), when (time), why (purpose), where (address), and how (method).

  3. **Execution**: This is a detailed explanation of how you desire to accomplish the mission.

  a. *Commander's Intent*

What is the leader's vision to connect the mission statement with the concept of the operation?

b. *Concept of the Operation*

   i. Scheme of maneuver

  ii. Formation

 iii. Route

 iv. Tactical missions to subordinate units

c. *Subunit Subparagraphs*

d. *Coordinating Instructions*

Specific instructions on how you plan on connecting to other friendly units (police, lawyers, judicial courts, and documents) with the mission

4. **Service Support:** This section explains the plan for food, equipment, uniforms, and weapons needed for this mission.

a. *Supply*

  i. Rations

 ii. Uniforms and equipment

 iii. Arms and ammunition

5. **Command and Signal:** This section identifies who is in charge of the mission and how you plan on communicating.

a. *Signal* - Frequencies and Call Signs

b. *Command* – Primary and Secondary

Format for an Executive Protection Strategy

I use the "Corporate Executive Protection" strategy template developed by Christian West & Brian Jantzen for long-term strategic planning. It normally has multi-layers and locations. The following is the format used as an executive protection strategy for a green energy CEO.

Introduction/Summary

* Statement of purpose – What are the reasons why you need this plan?

* Background: (Client)

* Background (Security)

* Objectives - What are you trying to achieve?

* Key success factors – What elements of the program are critical in order for it to be successful?

* Key performance indicators – What must be measured to ensure the plan is tracking?

Situational Analysis

* Risk, Threats, and Vulnerability Assessment

- External factors not in our control

- Internal factors in our control

Executive Protection Program Design

* **Who** is to be protected?

* **When** are the principals to be protected?

* **Where** are the principals to be protected?

* **What** kinds and levels of protection are necessary?

* **Why** is this protection needed?

Executive Protection Teams and Organization

* What are the key job descriptions and qualifications?

* How does this team interface with others in the organization?

* Training

Procurement Strategy

* For technology

* For human resources

Program Delivery and Maintenance

* What are the Standard Operating Procedures?

* How do we access security risks on an ongoing basis?

* How do we continually improve the skills of our staff?

Reporting and KPI Measurements

* Which KPI do we follow and measure?

* Which reports do we create on a regular basis?

Budget

* What are the program costs?

* What are the fixed and variable costs?

94

Implementation Plan

* Who has responsibility for implementing the program?

* Who has responsibility for moving the program forward?

Chapter 9: Self-Protection

On November 30, three kids were killed and eight were injured by a student at Oxford High School in Detroit. The tragic part is not that it's a tragedy in and of itself. The tragic part is that violence and horror are not new to us anymore. Violence has desensitized America to the point that we have become used to this occurrence as if it's the new normal. This is something that also applies to abuse and domestic violence. This is where I believe we need to become serious and alert the victims existing in this environment about the danger that they are in.

Based on my experience, when it comes to abuse, I do not support the shelter-in-place theory, especially in the era of Covid, where the abused may be forced to share their presence with their abusers. As time passes, many clients start trying to find logic and reasoning for their suffering. They think if the abuser is given some time to reflect, they will offer regret, calm down, and make amends for their action. But the pattern of behavior among abusers usually becomes serial by nature. They may tread lightly for a while, but ultimately anything may trigger the abuser to return to their primal state and repeat the aggression.

The National Coalition Against Domestic Violence[47] has identified early warning signs in the tension-building phase to immediately alert victims to *seek help* before the relationship becomes violent. Here are a few:

---

[47] Anon. n.d. "NCADV | National Coalition Against Domestic Violence." Retrieved January 18, 2022 (https://ncadv.org/).

- Extreme jealousy

- Possessive

- Threats

- A bad temper

- Animal cruelty

- Verbal abuse

- Extremely controlling behavior

- Antiquated beliefs about the roles of women and men in relationships

- Isolation from family and friends

- Blaming others for problems and feelings

If you notice a pattern where your partner is displaying some of these behaviors, that is a warning sign for you to realize these are the disturbances that will affect your life. Over 40 million guns were purchased in the year 2020. Shockingly, 46% of all the world's armed civilians live in the United States.

We are already facing the issue of gun violence as it is. The mass shooting epidemic shows no sign of slowing down. Now that things are returning to normalcy, people are returning to buy more deadly weapons, and the domestic violence situation is skyrocketing with it. Families try to find solace in the belief that the circumstances are temporary and that the situation will get better. But their predictions are unfounded, and things are simply not getting any better.

Options You Can Follow

So, my question is, where are we heading as a society? Are we going to go back to the record violence which occurred during the 1800s? During that time, colonists were required to own firearms to quickly mobilize a militia, to hunt, and to protect their livestock and home. Despite that mandate, only 13% of the 5.3 million colonists owned a firearm (approx. 690,000), yet the violence was out of control.

Are we heading back to the 1980s when a plethora of violent crimes peaked throughout America? Both scenarios are disastrous, yet both are occurring now. Violent crimes have matched the 1980s and we now have well over 393 million firearms in the USA. If this current trend persists without significant gun regulations, Americans will experience unmanageable carnage in our streets. Consequently, Americans will panic and buy even more guns. The result will be that owning and carrying firearms will become the new norm, and carrying that firearm will become as commonplace as carrying a cell phone. Is this the United States of America you wish to live in? I definitely do not and one of the reasons why I am sounding the alarm now!

Unfortunately, our civic politicians and law enforcement simply can't come to a rational agreement on how to respond to these threats. They can't develop a sound plan to mitigate these dangerous situations. For me, the situation is reaching a fever pitch, and it's already at a record level.

Hence, my reason for writing this book is that it is necessary to confront these issues. Do not be wary of Covid or the politics surrounding it. If you are, in fact, experiencing the early symptoms of abuse right now, you need to step up and act. You need to find shelter either in another household or in a help center. Because if you do not withdraw right now, your next altercation can become fatal.

Your first move must be to call 911 and demand the removal of the abuser. Remember that the law is on your side, so it is important to enter the courtroom with the right tools of protection in place for yourself. You must get a restraining order to legally document that the abuser remains as far away from you as possible. The order should state that the abuser will be committing a second-class felony and can be arrested if they contact you in any manner or is near your home. That information is easily enforceable by law enforcement or a protection team when necessary. Additionally, you must request the removal of firearms from the possession of the accused. Ask the judge for the removal or take it upon yourself to hand it over to law enforcement. The victim can also request that the judge requires the abuser to take anger management classes or counseling. All of this can be managed by the courts.

It is very important that victims pursue this course of action because of the growing presence of the gun violence rate in tandem with the domestic violence rate. The death rate will likely increase in the coming future. Much of the gun violence will be perpetrated within households by either the abuser or the abused, leading to more unnecessary deaths and traumas. When we currently have hundreds of deaths and injuries occurring from shootings every day, you can probably get the idea of how bad it is going to be when we go back to normal.

Unfortunately, there are other scenarios when the aggressor prevents the victim from seeking help from the authorities. In these situations, you must develop a strategy to deescalate the situation before planning your escape. You can make up a story of going to the gym, store, salon, or whatever it takes for you to leave that house. Once out, immediately contact the police, file a police report, and get them out of the house.

We Can Help

The facts are, if the abuser is beyond help, they will violate their restraining order, so calling 911 may not be helpful. If the person has a criminal record or history of violence and is on the street challenging you, you must seek additional help.

We specialize in keeping our clients safe while enforcing the court order against the abuser. Police officers are the response force, so do not expect them to remain in place if the abuser returns. They will write a police report and may look for the person, but that is not guaranteed. The situation is different for a security agency because your safety will be our only objective. We want the abuser to feel our presence. We will also confront the abuser preferably within 72 hours with the court order while photographing and videotaping the event. They will know that this incident can be used in court and they will be arrested by us if they are on the property. If they persist, we will do exactly that. Additionally, we encourage our clients to save all texts and emails, especially after the protection order has been served.

These texts and emails will become part of our final report and be provided to legal and law enforcement.

Chapter 10: Mission

With the number of domestic and gun violence skyrocketing and reaching unprecedented heights every day, in America, the mission can't be more clear. We must sound the alarm and provide conclusive, fact-based solutions for Americans to implement to avoid further casualties and deaths.

This book has identified three key objectives that can help accomplish this mission. These include:

1.   America has been subjected to countless acts of gun violence for far too long, and it's going to get worse. Therefore, owning firearms must now come with a greater sense of personal responsibility and consciousness. We must enact common-sense gun laws to strengthen our Second Amendment rights while making Americans safer and accountable. The Violence Project (<u>Mass Shooting Data & Research | The Violence Project</u>) identified five gun laws that can accomplish this before it further escalates.

2.   According to statistics, one in three women is subjected to abuse in America. In contrast, one in four men has become a victim of domestic violence. Victims in abusive relationships must act now and stand against the abuser. They must resolve this toxic environment by leaving it and filing a police report. Unfortunately, the data also shows that the risk of death and injuries increases exponentially if firearms are in the home.

3.   Communities plagued with domestic and gun violence cannot continue to wait for civic leaders and law enforcement

efforts to mitigate these threats. It will require a collective effort from the community to speak up against the violence and stand for a safe neighborhood. I believe revamping or establishing effective Neighborhood Watch and crime prevention programs is a viable solution. These programs can improve public safety and confidence with law enforcement.

It's time that we Americans stand united against all forms of violence, be it on women, men, children, sick or healthy, young or old, black, white, or differently colored, and take control of our streets. Security agencies and professionals must be prepared to provide countermeasures to help protect victims and secure our neighborhoods.